S0-CPB-273

RIDDLES
MALAPROPISMS
LITERALNESS CARRIED TO ABSURDITY
WORD FUSIONS

These are among the inventive forms of language that come out
of the mouths of children.

They can cause a chuckle.

They can produce puzzlement.

They can even make us angry when it seems that a child is
simply being "contrary."

What they actually are, however, are milestones on a child's
path to language skill development. Through hundreds of
examples, KIDSPEAK meticulously follows that path to show
parents how to more intelligently observe, encourage, and enjoy
this remarkable process, from the earliest forms of speech—
stringing sounds into sentences—to the mature use of language
as an effective life tool.

# KIDSPEAK:
# How Children
# Develop Language Skills

M. SUSAN BECK teaches English and Linguistics at the University of
Wisconsin, and makes her home in River Falls, Wisconsin. She is author of the
highly acclaimed *Baby Talk: How Your Child Learns to Speak,* also available in a
Plume edition.

# KIDSPEAK:
# How Children Develop Language Skills

M. Susan Beck

A PLUME BOOK
**NEW AMERICAN LIBRARY**
TIMES MIRROR
NEW YORK AND SCARBOROUGH, ONTARIO

NAL BOOKS ARE AVAILABLE AT QUANTITY DISCOUNTS WHEN
USED TO PROMOTE PRODUCTS OR SERVICES. FOR INFORMATION
PLEASE WRITE PREMIUM MARKETING DIVISION, THE NEW AMER-
ICAN LIBRARY, INC., 1633 BROADWAY, NEW YORK, NEW YORK
10019.

Copyright © 1982 by M. Susan Beck

All rights reserved

**Library of Congress Cataloging in Publication Data**

Beck, M. Susan.
    Kidspeak: how children develop language skills.

    Bibliography: p.
    Includes index.
    1. Language acquisition.    2. Semantics.
I. Title.
P118.B42    1983    401'.9    82-14518
ISBN 0-452-25376-4

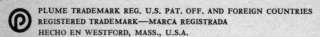

PLUME TRADEMARK REG. U.S. PAT. OFF. AND FOREIGN COUNTRIES
REGISTERED TRADEMARK—MARCA REGISTRADA
HECHO EN WESTFORD, MASS., U.S.A.

SIGNET, SIGNET CLASSICS, MENTOR, PLUME, MERIDIAN and NAL BOOKS
are published *in the United States* by The New American Library, Inc., *in Canada* by The
New American Library of Canada Limited, 81 Mack Avenue, Scarborough, Ontario
M1L 1M8.

First Printing, April, 1983

1 2 3 4 5 6 7 8 9

PRINTED IN THE UNITED STATES OF AMERICA

# Contents

# Preface

*Kidspeak* is the sequel to *Baby Talk,* published in 1978 by New American Library. In *Baby Talk,* I traced the process by and order in which children learn the elements of their native language, in this case, English. I presented the argument that children learn the sounds (or phonology) of the language, the word elements (or morphology) of the language, and the word order (or grammar) of the language in a predictable and orderly fashion as they mature from approximately eighteen months to six years of age. Finally, I suggested reading and writing projects that parents and elementary school teachers can use to increase children's sense of language.

What *Baby Talk* treated with less depth is the beginnings of children's sense of "meaning" in language. Ever since *Baby Talk* came out I have lectured, taught, and given speeches, and I have often been queried on the subject of how children learn language. Increasingly, the questions asked of me have to do with what children think language "means" and what they mean to say. Thus, *Kidspeak.*

*Kidspeak* attempts to explain how children discover that language is full of double meanings and ambiguities, and thus come to learn the skills they need to make up metaphors, invent jokes and riddles, tell stories, and express their peculiar sense of cause and effect, space and size—although they often err and produce unintentionally funny sayings.

Many acknowledgments are in order, but only some can be made by name. First, I would like to thank my numerous graduate students at the University of Wisconsin–River Falls, and their child subjects, who provided recorded data for this book during the last three years. Second, I would like to thank five mothers who carefully kept journals in which they recorded the language development of their children. They provided me with countless anecdotes, necessary to illustrate what might otherwise be too abstract. Those women are Patsy Lonie, Sue Bridewell Beckham, Lois Heilborn, Susan Koosman, and, most important, Lucinda Neuhous. Carole Hall served as an expert editor. Finally, I would like to thank my children, John Nicholas and Mary Ann, for understanding what I meant by "later" as they tried to give me space and time in which to write, and my husband, Robert, who helped to clear the cobwebs out of mind and matter and to whom this book is dedicated.

# PART I: A Theory of Meaning and of Child Development

# 1: The Doubleness of Language

For centuries people have raised questions about the nature of language and how it comes to be meaningful. How does it lend itself to our wish to express ourselves and command others? How does it relate us to the world of tangible things? How is it formed and transmitted from generation to generation and culture to culture? Such questions have engaged scholars through the literate ages of the western world. In fact, to some degree, to be a philosopher and to be a student of language was the same, and to be a student of language or a grammarian was to be a scholar. This was true in the days of Plato and Aristotle, during the period of the European Middle Ages and its development of palace schools, true even in the early part of this century.

The answers to questions about how language means, how it can effect behavior, how it can refer to a world of things, and how it is learned have differed in various times and among various thinkers. But one thing about our system of language seems generally to be agreed upon: Language is best understood if it is understood as a system of *doubles*. Language, as we use it, tends to do two things at once.

Language can cause us to behave in certain ways because it is a system that both signals *and* symbolizes. Furthermore, because language can symbolize, it can both name things that are there *and* enable us to contemplate, imagine, or in other ways think about things that are not there. Finally, language has a structure which both holds the symbolic words in place *and* is transmitted from generation to generation in a predictable order. Explaining just how this *duality* works is the purpose of this chapter.

In order to understand the development of meaning in child language, one must appreciate the significance of this duality. On one hand, language can signal, can name, and can provide a structure. These are all very explicit, easy-to-see functions. If one wants the door shut, one says "Shut the door," signaling through language a specific behavioral need. If one wants to teach a child or a non-native speaker a new word, one can say "This is a desk," naming the object that can also be pointed to, for it exists behind the word. If one wants to express oneself in English, one knows that certain words have to be spoken in a certain order for sense to be made.

On the other hand, language can symbolize, enabling us to conceptualize, and providing us with infinite possibilities of English expressions. These are less concrete functions, but they are crucial in the understanding of how we—as children and later as adults—manipulate this intricate system of sounds. For instance, chilled in front of an open door, one can think about the cozy fire of last winter, bemoan a rainy day, or envision the arrival of an expected visitor. Further, we are not limited to merely naming things in our environment. We can think about them in their absence and dream up pictures of the perfect desk for the library, a favorite desk with crystal knobs that sat on Mrs. Riley's porch, and more. Finally, once we have internalized the rules for the formation of the English sentence, we can create infinite combinations of words never before expressed; once we learn the rules of structure, we can be as creative in our expression as the rules will allow. This theory, that language is best understood as serving dual purposes, is at the heart of this book, and it is a theory for which I am largely in debt to Noam Chomsky, the well-known American linguist and philosopher.

As children learn language, they seem to learn its explicit functions first. They say "milk" and mean to command that someone give them a glass, or they say "milk" when naming the liquid in their glasses, or they say "milk gone" when expressing a condition that requires at least two words, put in the proper order. It is when they come to understand the less concrete functions of language that they seem to deepen their senses of what language can do and mean. It is at this later stage that they begin to make the metaphors, malapropisms, jokes, stories, and the like which are the subject of this book.

## Language as a System of Signals and Symbols

Whenever I give a lecture on the nature of language to my university students, I can anticipate a loud, fervent objection to one of the points I always make: that only human beings have language in the sense that language is a system of meaningful sounds by which we can communicate our wants, wishes, and understanding. Some recent studies of ape language would seem to counter my view. Eugene Linden, in *Apes, Men, and Language* (Penguin, 1976), summarizes some of the studies in which apes (the most famous are probably Sarah and Washoe) have been taught a kind of sign language which they use to communicate not only their basic needs for which all animals have signals, but expressive, emotional, and interpretive concerns. Whether these skills constitute "language" is still being debated; the evidence is also still out as to whether these learned skills will be passed on from ape generation to ape generation. Thus, I continue to suggest my point of view.

The objection is invariably from a student who loves his long-time pet and friend, the family dog . . . and the objection always is that Fido "understands" language and can "communicate." What this student fails to understand is that language, because of its double nature, can operate on the basis of signal and symbol.

In the case of Fido, his sound behavior is produced at the level of signal. That is, his sounds, or barks, are used to produce some kind of behavior on the part of another, to communicate a need, or to herald an activity. Most animals (and again I leave the debate about apes to others) are confined to live their lives as creatures of signal systems. Dogs bark to warn us of strangers approaching, of their hunger, of their feeling of threat and discomfort. Bees signal to one another the location of honey. Ants signal to one another, and with great alacrity, their finding of food. And so on.

We, too, are partly creatures of signal systems. We stop at red lights, we rise with an alarm clock, many of us dine at noon and at six whether we are truly hungry or not, we cease activity when we hear someone shout "Stop," we rise when the flag passes by in a parade, we answer the telephone when it rings. These responses to rather mechanical signals are part of the way we organize our daily lives.

Unlike lower animals, however, we are not simply creatures of signal systems; we are—by the definition of many scholars, philosophers, and psychologists—also symbol makers, and many of the forementioned would say that this is what defines us a human.

Because we are able to use symbols, especially those symbols that make up the complex system of language, we are able to do a great deal more than communicate our needs, desires, and demands for behavior from others. We can express ourselves, imagine and daydream, and create a special world that is uniquely our own.

What distinguishes a signal, which requires a response of some kind to be effective, from a symbol? The answer is partially built into the question. Signals require a physical or emotional or behavioral response; signals are immediate. For example, one can ignore a ringing telephone, but the expectation of the caller who signaled is that it will be answered right there and then. One can run a red light, but the expectation of the law is that the driver or walker will stop right there and then. One can refuse to join one's family for a six-o'clock dinner, but a sense of uneasiness often sets in when one realizes that the family's expectations have not been met and something has gone awry in the day's organization and pattern.

Symbols, on the other hand, are devices—often verbal, sometimes visual—which enable us to contemplate, to ponder, to wonder why. For example, because we are able to symbolize, we can remember a telephone call, just as we can rehearse one or work out a new dialogue for a disappointing one that we received and would like to have another crack at. We can think about "red" and conjure up fire, heat, or even ladies of the night. We can plan menus, project the success of a dinner party, and nostalgically review the favorite restaurant in which we secretly courted one another many years ago. Because we can act symbolically, we can think about things that are not currently there and that require no immediate action or response.

One of the most dramatic examples of the passage from signal behavior to symbolic sensibility is recounted by Helen Keller in her autobiography, a recollection staged and filmed as *The Miracle Worker*. For years and years, Helen Keller, a bright but blind, deaf, nearly mute child, could not learn, and could not be managed or "civilized," as her culture would have put it. Even under the tutelage of Annie Sullivan her progress was slow. Although the teacher tried and tried to teach Helen that a special sign language was a system of symbolic language, Helen continued to respond as a signal creature. She would sign the word for "doll" when she wanted Miss Annie to give her her doll; she would sign the word for "cake" when she wanted a piece of cake. She used this alternative language, this system of symbols, only to signal desired behavior on the part of someone else. Finally, after an eruption at the dinner table which Miss Annie forced her to amend by fetching water, she came to understand that the word for "water" did not simply signal to someone that water was needed; instead, the word was a name for something, a verbal symbol for something that she could talk about even when she didn't need its presence. She came to understand that language, whether signed or spoken, was a system of sounds and words that stood for or represented the objects, actions, feelings, and other contents of the world.

Less fortunate was Victor, famed as the wolf child in Truffaut's film *L'Enfant Sauvage* and diarized by his doctor, Dr. Itard, in *Wild Boy*. Victor had never been nurtured during the crucial days of language's beginning, the infant period of cooing and babbling. Although he learned to *communicate,* he never learned to *symbolize.* That is, he could respond to commands to get the milk or the hammer or the bowl and he could request that the milk, hammer, or bowl be got, but that was as far as he developed. Victor was unable to understand that the language he was learning was both a system that could signal behavior and a system that could symbolize one's sense of the world.

Because the words of our language are symbolic, they can be used to *name* the actual realities of our world and to *conceptualize* about those things and actions. This leads us to a consideration of another duality in language: It can denote or name things, actions, attitudes, and characteristics and it can lend itself to connotation or ideas about things, actions, attitudes, and characteristics.

## Language as Denotation and Connotation

However inefficient or impractical, words "mean" on two levels. They carry with them a denotative meaning and a connotative meaning. That is, they mean something to which we all pretty much agree, *and* they carry with them private pictures and images that are not always directly communicable. Because words carry connotations, we can see them in a very precise and particular way *and* we can see them as general categories for things.

One way to understand the denotation and connotation of words is to put a neutral word on a scale or ladder of abstraction, a term coined by a group of American linguists called General Semanticists and headed by S. I. Hayakawa. Since "desk" appeared earlier, it can serve again here. By "desk" we all mean about the same thing, i.e., a flat-topped object with four legs and, perhaps, some drawers. That is the word's general definition or denotation, but the word is not as neutral as it appears, for it lends itself as well to connotation and abstraction.

↑   *General*
    material goods
    household goods
    furniture
    **DESK**
    ebony desk
    ebony desk with crystal door pulls
    Mrs. Riley's ebony desk with crystal door pulls
↓   *Specific*

As we move up the ladder of abstraction, the meaning of "desk" becomes more and more general; as we move down, the meaning of "desk" becomes more specific, for the images, pictures, or connotations that the word produced finally indicate only one "desk."

Now what is it about language that lends itself to this kind of use? Granted, much of our language use is sheer communication. It operates as a system of signals to get a job done. Granted, much of our language is used to name and therefore be able to talk about the tangible world in which we live. But much of our language is also expressive. We daydream, we joke, we try to anticipate the future, we remember the past, we chat idly at cocktail parties. What is it in the nature of language that makes this possible?

Surely, one thing that enables language to perform so many functions is that it has a structure that enables it to be ordered and coherent, *and* it has content words which provide us with various meanings.

## Language as a Combination of Structure and Content

There are two classes of words in English. There are *content* words such as "ball," "run," "nice," and "quickly" that are otherwise called nouns, verbs, adjectives, and adverbs. There are also *structural* words which bear less clear meanings such as "the," "and," "or," "in," "of," and "on" (for instance, who ever saw a "the"?), but which, nonetheless, enable us to understand an utterance because they are signaling that a content word is coming up.

Consider a nonsense sentence such as this:

> The floog miralated in the spoggy mot.

None of us knows what this means in any precise way, but we all know that something called a "floog" is doing something called "miralating" in a place called a "mot," a place which is characterized as being "spoggy." We know this much because of the structural words which announce what is coming. Specifically, the word "the" announces that a noun is approaching; the *-ed* ending on a word announces that a verb is present; "in the" announces a noun phrase which, if a two-word phrase, more than likely contains an adjective and a noun.

Consider a nonsense sentence built on the reverse principle such as this:

> Floog fish swam spoggy mot wet swamp.

With the absence of "announcing" or structural words we can make no sense at all of this. Thus, structural words, although without any real world referent (there is no physical "the," "of," or "in" out in the tangible world), are crucial to our understanding of the meaning of an English utterance. These structural words are called *grammatical morphemes*. Their meaning is usually unambiguous, for they refer not to things in the experiential world, but to the form of an English sentence.

It is the *content* words which are of the most concern as one tries to understand the problems of communication, the power of poetry, the source of humor and error, or our ability to imagine and predict and remember. It is the content words which have experiential bases, which refer to things, actions, properties, and qualities in the real, tangible world out there. The references to the real world, however, are not the same for all of us; thus language expression becomes idiosyncratic, in part. Although, as a culture, we agree that words mean certain things—that "chair" refers to a four-legged piece of furniture, often with a back and arms, upon which one sits, and that "run" refers to an action of moving faster than one can when walking, an action that may involve hard breathing, sweating, and the wearing of tennis shoes—we don't always envision the exact same chair or movement as someone else. Some of us envision a velvet club chair when the noun is mentioned; some of us remember cramps in the calves when the verb is mentioned. Content words, in contrast to structural words, are often ambiguous because they refer to things, actions, and properties in the world that each of us experiences differently.

Content words have two general qualities. They express *conceptual* and *relational* properties. In the first case, content words have the qualities of inclusion, abstraction, ambiguity, restriction, and figurativeness. In the latter, content words have the qualities of synonymity, antonymy, and reciprocity. These terms sound formidable, but they describe qualities in our everyday use of language. Let us consider them one at a time, beginning with the *conceptual* properties of content words.

*Inclusion* is that quality of word meaning that enables us to understand that "color" includes "red *and* blue," that "organ" includes "heart *and* brain." Because some of our words include the meanings of other words we are able to *categorize*, a very important conceptual feat. If we were not able to categorize, our conversation and, in fact, world view would be a jumble of specific detail. We would have no verbal shorthand. Instead of being able to say that we love to live in a world of color, we would be forced to say that we love to live in a world of red, blue, yellow, green, orange, purple, and on and on. If we were not able to categorize, we would not be able to say that we love trees, but would have to express our affection for a certain kind of plant that has a gnarled trunk made of wood, branches with leaves of various kinds and colors, and seeds of various forms.

*Abstraction* enables us to speak very specifically about an antique wooden rocking chair with a quilted seat that was always to be found on Anna Johnson's porch, or talk about rocking chairs as a class, furniture in general, or household goods. As in this example, we can move from a very denotative, descriptive, specific statement about an object to a more open-to-interpretation, connotative, highly abstract statement that includes that earlier object.

*Ambiguity* is what produces "double meaning" within the context of our sentences. Thus, "She fed her dog biscuits" could mean that she fed biscuits to her dog or that she fed her female guest dog biscuits. The same principle underlies the confusion in the sentence "She enjoyed boring old ladies," which could mean that she enjoyed the company of old ladies who were boring or that she enjoyed being boring in the company of old ladies.

*Restriction* is the quality that disallows certain combinations of semantic features. For instance, the semantic features of "cat" include four-legged, furry, clawed, whiskered, and tailed. Thus, "The feathered cat is here" is not semantically sound. Likewise, "bachelor" has the semantic features of unmarried male. Thus, "The bachelor's wife looked in the mirror" is not an allowable combination of words.

Finally, and most importantly, content words have the conceptual quality of *figurativeness*. That means they can be metaphoric and vision-producing. Consider the earlier example of "desk," a "neutral" enough word. We all generally agree about what we mean by "desk" when we use the term. Yet, when the word is uttered, unless a specific desk is before our eyes, our vision varies from listener to listener; we each conjure up a specific desk that gives the word additional meaning. Because words prompt us to see in this way, we are also able to see relationships between things that share something in common. We see a color photograph of, say, Elizabeth Taylor, and note that her eyes are as violet as lavender sachet. We see a baby's pink-and-ivory face and remark that she looks like a china doll. We are able both to simply envision and to convert those images into metaphors because of the figurative power of content words.

The relational properties of content words are listed next. Note the interesting feature of each; to understand the meaning of one word, the speaker or listener must know the meaning of another word.

*Synonymity* is that quality of word meaning that enables us to vary our vocabulary in speaking of the same thing. Thus, we can eat or we can dine; we may be taught by a teacher or a professor; we may have an appointment with a doctor or a physician, an attorney or a lawyer.

*Antonymy,* on the other hand, enables us to speak in terms of opposites. Once we understand the meaning of "hot," we can understand "cold"; once we understand the meaning of "light," we can understand "dark." The list could go on: on and off, black and white, night and day, love and hate.

*Reciprocity* is a quality of word meaning that is somehow dependent upon the meaning of a closely related "other"; that is, some words have meaning only in relationship to a second word. For instance, we can buy something, but not without someone else who sells. We can eat, but—at least in the case of a child—not without being fed. We can drop something, but that something must go through the process of falling.

*Now,* children learn about the doubleness of language—and get very confused about it—from the time they're born until they're as old and sophisticated as we. Importantly, this learning is developmental; that is, they learn the nature of language bit by bit as they move from being signal makers to being metaphor makers.

# 2: The Child's Development of Meaning

This chapter outlines the common developmental patterns of children between the ages of two and kindergarten and shows how they come to know that language is a system of meaningful sounds that enables them to communicate, to express themselves, to imagine, and to create a verbal world in which they can govern their own experience. In order to learn language, young children must become aware of its "doubleness" as described in Chapter 1. They learn that language can be used to signal behavioral needs and to symbolize. They learn that language can both name a thing or an action and enable us to think about things and actions. They learn that language has a structure or grammatical form in which the content words of concepts and relationships lie.

## Learning Signals and Symbols

Infant children, until they are approximately eighteen months old, are learning the sounds of the English language. They begin by unwittingly babbling and cooing. Then, partly by nature and partly by nurture, they learn that sounds like *a* are different in kind from sounds like *p* (since the former is a vowel and the latter a consonant). They learn, although they do not bring this knowledge to any level of consciousness, that English is a system of vowels and consonants. They learn, too, that by moving their tongues around and varying their breathing, they can produce vowels that differ from one another, as *a* differs from *i*. The same thing is true of their learning consonant variations, their learning that *p* and *t* are different from one another. After playing with the thirty-six sounds native to English, they start producing their first recognizable words, such as "baba," "mama," and "dada," which sound to an adult listener like "baby," "mommy," and "daddy." The first sounds children learn are those that are the easiest to produce, the sounds produced in the front of the mouth (*p, b, d, t, m, n*), which require the least tongue and air control. Thus, a baby's first words are very likely those that his or her ecstatic parents think are spoken: "mama, papa, baba, dada, nana."

To be emphasized here is that these first efforts at language are unwitting. The child hasn't the cognitive skills yet to realize that she is trying to do anything at all.

Eventually, the child comes to know at an uncertain level of consciousness that certain combinations of vowels and consonants produce sounds that, in turn, produce *action* and *behavior* on the part of another. The year-old child somehow knows that the combination of vowels and consonants in the word "milk" may well produce a glass of milk for her consumption, that the utterance of "up" may well produce the act of being lifted, and that "book" may well produce the act of being read to.

At this point of language development, however, the child is little different from her favorite puppy whose sharp bark may produce a watchful eye on the driveway in fear of intruders, whose less alarming bark may produce a bowl of food, whose whimpering may cause its entry into the warmth of the house on a blizzardy winter evening. The child is using what she knows about language, as Fido uses his barking, to *signal* a need or desire to someone whom she wishes to act on her behalf.

Nonetheless, children, without dramatic insight or life-long frustrations, come to understand that the language they're learning is both a system that can signal behavior *and* a system that can symbolize one's sense of the world, a system that they can use, even in infancy, to name objects, order actions, make comments, and make requests.

For example, even year-old children who somehow know that "milk" may well produce a cold glass of milk can also say "milk" when they mean to comment that it is spilled, that the cat licked it up, or that it tastes funny. Obviously, one must be physically present to hear the child's comments in order to know what meaning is intended, for the child, who in infancy usually utters only one word at a time, has no context in which her intended meaning could be clear.

Children learn very early, then, that words not only elicit action, that words not only name things, but that words can be used to comment upon the world and to evaluate that world and to express themselves about an attitude held toward some part of the world. Even in infancy, as our children learn language, they are learning about meaning and symbol making.

What the infant child has been learning is the sound system of English, called, by those of us who are self-conscious about language, *phonology*. Phonology is the study of the process by which native speakers come to understand that certain sounds are permissible in English and that certain combinations of sounds are not. Although infants can produce all the sounds of known languages, they become selective, finally, and English-speaking children quickly reject such combinations as *gkb* while accepting such combinations as *str* in words like "strike."

There are other levels of language that children must learn, as well. English is a language that is dependent upon word order for meaning. We simply cannot mix up nouns, verbs, adjectives, and adverbs and hope that our intended meaning will be understood. Instead, we internalize a pattern by which nouns are preceded by adjectives and followed by verbs which are, in turn, followed by adverbs (most of the time). This understanding is the beginning of an understanding of *syntax* or *grammatical rule,* which begins when the child is over two and gains sophistication as the child enters kindergarten.

English has another element in its construction. If we create a sentence such as "Bird fly high" or "Sally eat lunch?" we, as adult speakers, know that something is missing, something is awry. We have learned, as our three-year-olds do, that English has little words or parts of words that make a difference in what we mean when we speak. Three-year-olds learn a great deal about those little words or parts of words as they make a study, however unconscious, of what we call *morphology*. They learn to use "the," "a," "in" and "on," the *'s,* the plural *s,* the *-ing* verb form, and two forms of the past tense verb (*-ed* as in "walked" and vowel change as in "sing, sang, sung").

By the time children are four or five, they have put these levels pretty much together and are developing on the level of meaning or *semantics.*

## Learning Language Structure and Content Words

As children mature to two years or thirty months, their approximately one-hundred-word vocabulary begins to be used in a new way. No longer content to merely utter single words as sentences that are wide open to interpretation, two-year-olds start putting two words together, making primitive adult sentences.

These two-word sentences reveal the level of meaning that the child has developed. For instance, he learns that words can be used to express qualities and/or to describe. He learns that "blue" is such a word and says "blue ball." Children learn that words can be used to express ownership or possession, and they say "Mommy lunch." They learn that some words refer to people in action (doers) and that some words refer to the action those doers perform or create, and they say "Sally read."

The two-year-old is learning that language has a structure *and* that it has content words simultaneously in these examples. In the first case, the two-year-old is working out the task of learning the elementary rules of word order in English. She is learning how English is structured by using language in an attempt to get the agent/action/object/location pattern of the normal English sentence down pat. She is heading for a string of words such as "Johnny took the blue truck home."

I will elaborate by example. Our two-year-old can produce "Johnny truck," indicating that the truck is Johnny's; she can produce "truck home," indicating location; she can produce "blue truck," indicating quality. What she can't do is to produce all the parts at once. But notice what is important. The sentence elements that she produces are *always* in the right order.

Two-year-olds are learning about the use of content words, also, although children are generally denotative in their use of such words. That is, they know to what the words "ball," "run," "nice," and "quickly" refer and they use such words to name, describe, and specify a present object, action, or property. They comment about the ball right in front of them, their own nice puppy, and the quick running of their parent. They are still far from the knowledge that "ball" is a noun that belongs in the larger category of "toys" or that "ball" can be used figuratively in a phrase such as "round as a ball." They have not yet learned that "run" belongs in a larger category such as "movement," or that "run" can be used figuratively in reference to a damaged pair of panty hose which has "runs" in it. They have not yet learned that the content words of English can do more than denote or name. They have not yet learned that the content words of English are ripe with conceptual and relational meanings that enable us to categorize, abstract, make metaphors, and discuss relationships.

Two-year-olds, in fact, are at a very limited stage of knowing how language "means." They use their vocabulary in very direct ways—to name, to show possession, to locate, to describe, and the like—and the order in which they place their words indicates what they mean. Insofar as they depend upon word order for meaning, they are still syntactically or grammatically bound. Their meaning is bound, in part, to the order in which they place content words.

This is even more true of the three-year-old. Three-year-old children stop sounding like miniature telegram readers, for their linguistic task is to learn about the little words and parts of words in English that linguists call grammatical morphemes and that I've been calling structure words. They learn that the ball does not only roll, but that it roll*s* and *is* roll*ing*. They learn that the ball can be multiple and can belong to someone special, and they say that "the balls are Johnny's." They learn that time is indicated in verbs and say that Mommy sings in the choir or that she sang in the choir Sunday. They are, however, more attracted to the ease of the "walk, walked" kind of verb and are thus inclined to say that Mommy "singed" on Sunday. The task of acquiring the grammatical morphemes of the language is an enormous one, the importance of which is best demonstrated by example.

If one were confronted with a sentence made up entirely of nonsense words where English content words (nouns, verbs, adjectives, and adverbs) should be, one could still guess at the suggested meaning of the sentence. In fact, Lewis Carroll's "Jabberwocky" is a prime example of this very thing. Consider again this sentence, a variant of which appeared earlier:

> The floogs miralated in the flastic bog.

Because "the" indicates that a noun is coming, and nouns inflect for plurality by the addition of an *s,* and verbs form the past tense by the addition of an *-ed* ending, and "in the" suggests a noun phrase or prepositional phrase to follow, we can guess that this sentence is commenting about more than one thing doing something in a particular place.

If we substitute nonsense words for the grammatical morphemes (the little words and parts of words) rather than for the content words, we are in big trouble. Consider this sentence:

> Floogs birds scrambled miralate flast damp ground.

In this case, we can guess at no meaning, because the sentence has no context; the clues it should provide to us are missing.

That three-year-old children learn all this is amazing at least.

Children from birth to the age of nearly four, then, are awfully busy learning the essentials of the English language—its sounds, its rules of word formation, and its rules of word order. What they use this information to do is quite limited. They generally speak to request something, to name something, to comment on the condition of something, and to ask simple questions.

It is probably self-evident that children do not acquire the adult-level sense of word and language meaning as quickly as they learn the order of word formation and word order. Until they are five or six years old, they don't consciously understand the conceptual and relational qualities of content words. They are more interested in the order of words in an utterance (the syntactic meaning of a sentence) and the denotative meaning of each word. They are still not quick to categorize, to abstract, and generally to see the connections between things. They do not yet have a conscious sense of the paradigmatic nature of language, of its double abilities, of its ability to categorize, abstract, relate, connote, and the like.

That most preschool or even kindergarten children do not have this understanding of the paradigmatic level of language can be seen in their early errors. They try to catch on, but until they are around six years old, some, if not all, of these content word qualities are beyond them. For example, a child may try to categorize, but her overgeneralizations are often disordered. Thus, the child will understand that a dog is a four-legged animal and then proceed to call larger four-legged animals, such as cows, "big dogs." Synonymity rarely occurs to the very young child, because her vocabulary is limited to around 200 words (by the age of three). The child faced with situations that require an understanding of antonymy is often confused, for her ability to categorize is still limited. The child who is able to respond fully to a "word-association" test is rare. Because the young child is still syntactically organized in her use of words, she is inclined to respond to a given word, not in terms of its own meaning, but in terms of the kind of word she expects to follow. To be specific, if one asked a young child to respond to the word "shiny," her likely response would not be "dull," but might be "truck," since she knows that words like "shiny" signal that a noun with that quality will probably follow. An actual example of such error turned up on a readiness test given to pre-kindergartners at a local school. The children were asked to fill in the blank in this series: "breakfast, lunch, _____." The answer looked for was, of course, dinner or supper, but one little boy replied "tuna fish," which was as close a response to "lunch" as he could think of.

Reciprocals, too, give children a lot of trouble. Fortunately, English doesn't have too many of them. Philip Dale in *Language Development: Structure and Function* (Holt, Rinehart & Winston, 2nd ed., 1976) cites some funny examples. A little girl reputedly told her mother "not to eat the baby yet. She's too smelly." Another child "falled the cup."

About the young child's sense of the other four qualities of content words—abstraction, ambiguity, restriction, and figurative power—we know very little. The young child, until she's at least four, doesn't have enough power of expression to give us clues to the "pictures" in her mind that would reveal her sense of abstraction or the figurative power of words. The qualities of restrictivity and ambiguity seem not to trouble the young child, for it is the preschool child in particular who seems to delight in stories, especially those of Dr. Seuss, that break every such rule. For instance, the phrase "green eggs" denies our restriction rules. In a study conducted by David McNeill and recounted in *The Acquisition of Language: The Study of Developmental Psycholinguistics* (Harper & Row, 1970), preschool children responded to the following sentences in pretty much the same way; although only the first is sensible, they found *both* quite entertaining and appropriate, since they didn't know the meaning of any of the words anyway, but the structural signals were all in order:

The wild elephants climbed up the rocky hills.
The ticking elephants shot up the old elevator.

At a slightly older age, the child moves away from such total dependence upon syntactic structure as a signal for meaning and begins to pay more attention to content words and their potentials for meaning. In a semantic study summarized by McNeill, seven-year-old children were given a test to see if they depended upon word order (syntax) or word meaning (semantics) for the interpretation of something they had heard. Younger children, the reader will remember, are almost always more attached to the order of words than they are to the semantic content of those words. Seven-year-old children apparently are most concerned to keep the semantic or content part of an utterance sensible, even if that means letting go of a syntactic form. To illustrate, seven-year-olds were asked to listen to or read these sentences:

> The bird is inside the cage.
> The cage is under the table.
> The bird is yellow.

When questioned later, they accepted as "true" the statement "The bird is under the table," but rejected "The cage is over the table." Unlike younger children, who in all likelihood would have accepted both because the word order so closely resembled the sentences they had heard, older children opted for the "truth" of semantic meaning, depending less upon the message delivered by appropriate word order or sentence form.

What can the researcher, teacher, student, or parent learn from the mistakes children make while they are learning their native tongue?

To consider this in developmental order, return to the infant child. The child who cannot master such difficult sounds as *g* or *k*, difficult because they are formed way back in the throat and require a great deal of tongue and air control, will not substitute just any sound for the one he cannot make. Instead, the child will approximate the missing sound by substituting one that is most like it (formed nearby, for instance as is *d* or *t*, or sharing other qualities of sound). Thus the child who cannot ask for a scissors to *cut* something will ask for a scissors to *tut* something; the child who cannot express glee over the Cookie Monster can show his appreciation for the Tookie Monster.

The three-year-old who has learned the complicated system of verbs in English and, early in his third year, has learned the differences between "sing" and "sang," "ran" and "run," will suddenly come upon yet another kind of verb system, represented by the verbs "walk" and "walked," and begin using that pattern for everything. He will say, regardless of parental correction, that "Mommy singed in the choir" and that "Johnny runned home."

What this suggests is that while children learn this complex system we call language, they are demonstrating that they learn by seeking out *patterns* and *rules* for language formation.

Even very young children who err in the production of sound seem to sense that there are patterns and rules for sound formation, that certain sounds, such as front consonants, have something in common that back sounds do not share, and when they make substitutions, they attempt to approximate as closely as possible the pattern they cannot yet reproduce. When children convert all verbs to the "walk, walked" variety, they are overgeneralizing a rule that they have become comfortable with. When children accommodate what they hear to what they know, they are nonetheless keeping within the pattern of sounds and meaning they have learned.

Noam Chomsky has developed an extensive theory of the relationship of language learning to learning in general, and he, too, would argue that a child learning language is a child learning patterns that are based on rules and forms that we, as native speakers, rarely bring to consciousness—and, most important, their learning of these patterns is not something that they copy or mimic. They are active, creative experimenters with the elements of language and learn that language on terms that make sense to them and seem to follow some unnamed but sensed rule.

In the following chapters we'll see how the school-age child moves beyond a dependence on sentence form for meaning (what I have been calling syntactic meaning) and develops a sense of the importance of the qualities intrinsic in content words (paradigmatic meaning). We shall look at this learning of semantics or meaning and see that once children learn to recognize ambiguity and literal and figurative meaning, they enter the world of poetry and metaphor, humor, storytelling, and reading, all of which are addressed in this text.

# PART II: *The Learning of Concepts and Relationships*

# 3. The Child as Metaphor Maker and Poet

When some people hear the word "poetry," they shudder, remembering too well the rote memorization of so-called classics in an eighth-grade English class, adolescent attempts to write love sonnets rhyming "love," "glove," and "dove," or their wonderment as college students that anyone would really care whether or not Milton had lost his Paradise.

Yet, poetry is, in a special way, natural to all of us, and we produce at least two forms of it on a regular basis by comparing one thing with another and by participating in the jargon or slang of our time.

Anytime we try to express our sense of a thing, experience, or emotion in terms of another thing, experience, or emotion which we assume our listeners share, we are approaching the use of metaphoric language. When we say that a new dress is "grass-green," we are comparing the known quality of green grass to the yet unseen color of the new dress. When we say that our hands are as "cold as ice," we are comparing the shared sense of frozen water to the condition of our hands. The comparison of a known quality to an unknown or difficult-to-express quality is a kind of metaphor. The problem with most of our comparative expressions is that they are tired; they are clichés; they have staled and paled with overuse.

It is the rare user of language among us who would see a swarm of birds and note that together they look like a large, dotted fish; or wish to describe a new leaf and note that it is as green as winter wheat in April after a spring rain; or describe a barren tree after an ice storm by referring to its clinking and glistening as "crystal." This kind of language creation is generally left to our professional makers of metaphor, our poets.

Some of our conversational poetry is less stale and tired, although it is quickly dated. This conversational invention of language is commonly called "slang," and, in its way, it is everyman's poetry. Anyone who knows a real "turkey" who habitually gets "bombed" and then assumes himself to be "mellow and all laid back" knows something about common parlance and its relationship to poetry, for behind even these simple examples exists an actual stupid, awkward bird which we call a turkey, the notion of destruction, and the visual image of relaxation. Again, this comparison of a physical condition to tangible objects, things, and events constitutes the metaphoric use of language.

Children, too, make their experience sensible through the invention of metaphor. As children attempt to understand and to interpret their universe, they, too, relate what they know to what is new to them, and the result is often inventive, poetic, and metaphoric language.

A caution is in order. Children do not invent language all the time, nor are their inventions always worth recording in the baby book. More often than not, when one asks a child what she's learning in school, the answer will be "stuff" or "things" or "nothing." But once in awhile our children enable us to see the world with new eyes because their untired ones, their fresh ones, their unused ones do connect with their voices to produce special expressions that are meaningful for all of us.

A reminder is in order too. Children do not invent language, in the metaphoric sense, at just any age or stage of their development. In the process of learning this complicated system called the English language, children pass through various stages that are akin to their physical and cognitive development, described in Chapter 2.

To recall, it is not until children are nearly four that their interest in simply naming and commenting about objective things and actions seems to dim. They begin, instead, to wonder. They increasingly ask questions about the whys, hows, and whens of their experience. They encounter experiences—whether through play or day school or family outings—that are new to them. They begin to *interpret,* rather than merely *comment* on their own experiences, and this marks the real beginning of their metaphoric production of language, metaphors whose sources tend to be sensual or mechanical. That early metaphor or "poetry" is sensual in nature is not surprising. That it is also often mechanical is harder to explain.

Four-year-old children maintain earlier linguistic habits and intentions. Just as infant children use single-word sentences to name and describe objects, and as two-year-old children combine words to describe the nature of a ball or dolly or truck, and as three-year-old children continue to specify and describe, four-year-old children are also creatures of their senses. They are concerned with the smell of a thing, the touch of a thing, the look of a thing, and the sound of a thing. What is special about four-year-old children, however, is that their sensual awareness begins to take on *conceptual* dimensions. They begin to notice function or use and they begin to see comparatively. That is, they begin to see objects and live through experiences which are no longer isolated and discrete. They come to see relationships between several objects and/or several events, and in comparing one to the other, they are learning the principle of *categorization.* They are learning that certain kinds of similarities (such as "four-leggedness") enable them to form groups or types (such as "animal"). They learn, too, about metaphor when they come to realize that they can express their feelings and attitudes about a new object or event in terms of one that is already understood and experienced.

These generalizations are best illustrated by actual examples of four-year-old metaphoric or poetic speech. A child, fond of fruit and sensitive to the colors of its ripeness, looked out the window one very late evening and remarked that it was "as dark as a plum." As adults, we are so prone to cliché that our expression would more than likely have been "It's pitch-black." Yet, there is a purple, plumlike quality to evening darkness that our eyes have been blinded to and our mouths muted from commenting upon.

A child, in telling a story about favorite games and sports, was trying to explain what he understood about the rules of football. When asked what a football looked like, he replied, "It's sort of an oval shape with two corners." Again, as adults, we would connect with its oval quality and assume that we were understood. Yet, this child knew that the points of the ball made it different from an egg-shaped object and described those points with the reference to a similar geometric form, i.e., the corner.

Another child, obviously a fan of television's Mr. Whipple, sat upon her uncle's lap and after fondling his bearded face, remarked that he had a "Charmin beard," a metaphor that was also a play on words. The beard was soft and squeezable; it was also "charming."

Traumatic events often produce metaphoric expressions based on the similarities of experiences. A young girl was bitten by a bumblebee and vividly remembered her discomfort. On a walk, she brushed into a prickly bush and said, "Oh, that's a bumblebee plant."

Children seem, at four, to be particularly confused about the physical functions of their own bodies. Thus, their expressions of bodily sensation are rich with metaphor. A child, after a long and apparently exhausting walk, exclaimed that she "got a heartbeat," her way of describing shortness of breath and palpitations. The same child was trying to explain the experience of nearly choking while swimming and said, "I swallowed my mouth with water." A special sense of physical function is also present in this expression, produced after a young girl became aware that she had burped. Her explanation was that her "cough popped." A young boy became aware of his own nakedness while bathing and said, with some embarrassment, "Look at me. I'm barefoot all over." Another child commented upon the taste of a mint in his mouth. His interpretation of its strong, but pleasant, flavor was "I have a breeze in my mouth."

Children do not always construct metaphors from the sensual sources of color, shape, texture, and other sensations. They are also creatures of the industrialized twentieth century, and the mechanical objects around them serve as additional sources for their imaginations. At one time, poets used the symbols of nature to explain human emotion or to describe human events (e.g., "Her eyes are as reflective as the moon"). Today's children also tend to explain the functions of human and animal nature through comparisons with machines. Three such examples follow:

A child, describing the activities of various animals, referred to the dog's barking as "honking" and to a frog's breathing as the frog "blowing up his stomach with a pump."

As parents, we all remember those deplorable toys that well-meaning friends presented to our young children—plastic lawn movers that went clickety-click at ever increasing noise levels, schoolhouses with bells that actually rang, toy telephones that groaned their numbers and jarred our ears. In the early years of one child's life, those toys were relegated to an upstairs playroom, well out of the sight and hearing of parents. The child, like his favorite toys, was also very noisy, chattering endlessly as he ran about. Realizing one day that his chatter was annoying his mother, he remarked that his "mouth was an upstairs toy."

A young girl had just lived through the experience of her father finishing his doctoral degree and, of course, completing the inevitable task of writing his dissertation. She awakened one evening, came downstairs where her father was working, and commented that her chattering teeth were "typing."

Yet, children don't respond with much sense to adult metaphors or everyday clichés. A kindergarten class was asked to respond to a series of adult clichés, a response that the teacher hoped would reveal their sense of meaning. The following phrases were given to the children:

1. Keep your nose to the grindstone.
2. You're pulling my leg.
3. You're all thumbs.
4. Get off my back.
5. Lend an ear.
6. Use some elbow grease.
7. You put your foot in your mouth.
8. Stick together through thick and thin.
9. You're short-sighted.
10. You crack me up.

To "Keep your nose to the grindstone," the children responded, "Keep your nose out," "Keep your nose to yourself and don't keep it to other people," "You like to smell it," "You put a stone in your hand and then you put your nose down to your hand or if you're outside you can put your nose to the ground," "Cover your nose when you sneeze."

Most of the children had a sense that "You're pulling my leg" had something to do with teasing, but some children said that it meant "You're trying to pull my leg off," and one child simply said "Ouch."

"You're all thumbs" baffled many of the children, who either didn't respond or responded with these phrases: "All messed up," "You're all over thumbs," "Their whole body is thumbs," "You like thumbs," and, my favorite, "All children are thumbs because they're small."

To consider two more items should suffice for a generalization. When asked to respond to what "putting your foot in your mouth" meant, the children said, "You're a baby," "Put your toe in your mouth," "Be quiet," "Your mouth is big," and "You should take off your shoes and socks and put your foot in your mouth."

When asked to explain what "sticking together through thick and thin" meant, the children made these responses: "Stand still and tight together," "When you're talking to someone it means don't fall apart on your words," "Means one is fat and the other is skinny and they're going to stay together," "It means kind of like quicksand," and "Putting tape on both of them."

The point here is rather simple. Although four-to-five-year-old children are capable of producing marvelous metaphors and poetic observations of their universe, these productions are still quite *unintentional*. They are, when asked to *intentionally* interpret something, such as the adult clichés, still literal-minded. They are not yet secure with the world of double meanings, the world of denotative and connotative language. But this will develop.

What has preceded is a brief chronicle of examples that show that children use their senses and their sense of mechanics to make sense of their world. Parents who often record the precious utterances of their children frequently get distressed when these metaphoric utterances stop. The apparent stopping point of a child's creativity or language invention seems to parallel the child's entry into school. This heralds outcries from parents who are concerned already about what the schools are doing to their little geniuses. What happens to school-age children, in terms of their sensitivity to language, can only be addressed theoretically, but what seems to happen is twofold: They learn to read and they shift gears in their invention of language.

Preschool children, once they have a significant enough vocabulary to make lively comparisons between the sensual characteristics of one thing and the characteristics of another, seem to have no sense of so-called "right" or "correct" meanings for words. They are experimenting with meaning and its role in full communication. They cannot read or use dictionaries; thus, their language is not locked into any level of literary expectation.

School children, on the other hand, learn to read, learn to look up hard words, make spelling lists complete with definitions, and are regularly drilled on word relationships such as those that exist between synonyms, antonyms, and reciprocals.

Granted, the approaches to reading and vocabulary building are sure to vary from school to school, teacher to teacher, and grade level to grade level, and each approach has virtue. Many elementary school curricula are designed with a real sense of what the child already knows about language, i.e., its grammar, its sounds, its rules for word formations, and its openness to being played with. Those curricula have some sense of the psycholinguistic needs of the child, a sense that a child's learning abilities and language development are related. In teaching reading, the children are encouraged to immerse themselves in the printed page as though they were acquiring a second language, to connect printed words with meanings and ideas, and to connect those ideas with their own experience and to comprehend the nature of the story or text.

In teaching vocabulary building and writing, some teachers often employ the language-experience approach with their elementary students, an approach which asks students to recite their own stories, which are then written down, made into little books, and used as class materials.

In both these briefly summarized situations, what the child already knows about language is respected, as is her creativity and ability to develop appropriate language forms.

Although I am no expert in reading or reading theory, I have become concerned about what seems to happen to children's creativity upon entering school with a curriculum less enlightened in its approach to reading and vocabulary development. Considered here are just two rather distressing examples of rigid instruction which seem in the first case to separate sound from sense and in the second to overemphasize "correctness."

A popular method of teaching reading is a method that teaches children to "decode"—that is, to learn to recognize and pronounce a word and/or a word element. For instance, children will be introduced to the word "ill." They are then asked to decode words related in formation to "ill," such as "Jill," "hill,"

"Bill," "hilly," and "will." Notice that it is the word *formations* that are similar, not their *semantic* content. The notion of being sick has nothing to do with proper nouns, mounds of earth, or perseverance. Children who may want to be reading about *Star Wars* are now equipped to read a short tale about Jill and Bill going up the hill and against their will becoming ill. Although children can decode these kinds of word formations, they have learned nothing about their semantic connection to one another, the early source of their metaphoric constructions. They can read all the right words, but they are not emotionally or imaginatively involved in what they're reading about.

The emphasis on right words and the right meanings for words becomes painfully clear in terms of restrictions on the child's sensibilities if one examines commercially produced worksheets on word relationships.

Gleaned from such an actual worksheet are these samples:

The children in a third-grade class were asked to give the opposites for a list of words, each of which had a "right" answer that, in some cases, seemed arbitrary at best. Some words and their "correct" pair made good child and adult sense. "Cold" required "hot"; "buy," "sell"; "under," "over." But some were certainly more open to interpretation, an interpretation that was not encouraged.

Consider the remainder of the list, which included the words "some," "call," "rip," and "solid." Any one of us could pair up "some" with "few," "many," or "none"; could pair up "call" with "answer," "respond," even "echo"; could pair up "rip" with "untorn"; could pair up "solid" with "liquid." Yet, the "right" answers were these: "few," "answer," "mend," and "flimsy." This is capricious and forces the school-age child to think of language as being somehow right and wrong as the child uses it. This would seem to limit the child's attempts at self-expression and increase the child's concern for simple correctness.

Much of what has preceded might suggest that reading and language invention are at odds with one another. Not at all!

Part III will illustrate the degree to which I hold reading and language development as handmaidens of one another. Even at this juncture, it should be emphasized that reading books reinforces phonological rules (although English spelling is notorious for being nonphonetic), morphological rules concerning the importance of little words and parts of words such as plurality and possession, and the importance of consistent word order. Moreover, reading introduces new vocabulary and heightens the child's awareness of the kinds of things that can be expressed.

The relationship between learning reading and the reduction of spontaneous language invention seems to be of another order. If one assumes that learning to read is like learning another symbolic system or "language," then this relationship can perhaps be understood. Wanting to be correct in the acquisition of a kind of second language, children tend to put their first one at abeyance. They temporarily freeze it, since it has been learned and is theirs.

Soon, however, the world that opens to them through reading creates a shift of gears in language invention, as mentioned earlier. Their vocabulary enriched, the power of words revealed, they begin to create language again, but on the basis of what they think they've heard, not what they think they've sensed. This is the subject of the next chapter.

# 4: The Child and Malapropism: Is Hearing Really Understanding?

School-age children continue to invent language. Although their eyes may be trained on reading books and worksheets, their auditory skills and imagination seem to enable them to shift gears in their language inventiveness. What school-age children seem to do is to continue to invent language, but their principle of invention changes. They are no longer as apt to relate physical characteristics to one another, as they did as younger children, but now relate *sound* similarities to one another. The essential point is that children's capacity to invent language, to explore their universe creatively on their own linguistic terms, does not necessarily diminish as they mature. What seems to happen is that they mature from a purely sensual metaphoric sense (such as "The night is as dark as a plum," in which physical qualities are used poetically) to a sense of word meaning based on sound relationships which produces a special new vocabulary for them. It's as though children hear what we say, or see what they read, or repeat something they're supposed to learn—but then say to themselves, "Did I hear that right?"

The special vocabulary they begin to produce is a vocabulary full of unintentional errors, many of which are very funny indeed. The errors tend to be of a particular kind. They are *malapropisms,* named for Mrs. Malaprop, a character in Richard Sheridan's play *The Rivals* who never repeated anything she heard quite in the way it was said. More contemporary examples of the humorous use of malapropisms can be seen in the television language of Archie Bunker.

Like metaphors, malapropisms are the child's attempts to make language meaningful in terms that he or she can understand, and they occur in all areas of children's endeavors. They produce malapropisms as they try to increase their vocabularies to resemble more closely the vocabulary of adult speech. They create this new vocabulary when they try to understand what is going on in school or in their music lessons. They invent when they try to understand what a parent does at work. They create, too, when they are taken into a new environment.

Most parents have carefully preserved such language inventions of their school-age children. Some anecdotes are included here to illustrate the generalization that children are little Mr. and Mrs. Malaprops.

Efforts to talk like an adult produce some interesting combinations and restructuring of English word elements. An older grade school girl, after pleading for months for a curly permanent, was given one. Suddenly, she wasn't so sure she loved it. Knowing the words "radiant" and "idiotic," her two extremes for the potential results of the perm, she asked her mother if she looked "radiotic." The same girl and her neighbor had been given possession of an extra room in the former's home, a room that was to be used for crafts, studying, gab fests, or anything else reasonably sensible, on the condition that the room be kept in order. Posted on the door to that room appeared this sign:

> Tracy has asked Mary Ann to be a part of her room. Mary Ann said yes! But Tracy must now take participance in it.

A seven-year-old boy was diligently working on a crossword puzzle when his mother interrupted his concentration. Knowing that something had happened to his "train of thought," as an adult would probably have put it, he said, in some disgust, "Mom, you broke my mind."

The errors in reproducing adult speech in instances when the word in question is particularly specialized or polysyllabic are also rampant. A seventh-grade boy was watching his mother seal Christmas cards with a seal—or embosser—that imprinted her initials. Intrigued by the process, he inquired about what she was doing and then volunteered to "help her embalm the cards." This same child was reading a newspaper and saw an ad for something that cost $2,000. Child of the electronic age that he is, he commented that with that kind of money, he could buy eight Ataris and, if he were an octopus, he would then "have one for every testicle."

On one occasion an uncle took a favorite nephew on a long camping trip into Canada. Enroute, they experienced car trouble, and had to push the vehicle down a small hill in order to get it going again. The uncle steered; the nephew pushed. After leaping back into the now-moving car, Charles exclaimed, "I've never been so humidified in my life." To this day, the young man's family thus refers to their humidifier as the "humiliator." This same boy was telling ghost stories at one of the encampments. He got to the inevitable crux of the tale—where the old maid looks under her bed to find something horrifying, something that could well make her hysterical—and said that the old maid had turned into "a historical sight."

A seven-year-old boy, after receiving a shock in his home merely from touching metal, was told something about "static." He now refers to static as "an electric irritator."

When children try to come to terms with what they are learning in school they also produce these wonderful expressions called malapropisms. A seven-year-old was taking violin lessons and learning a piece called "Allegro." Even many of us don't know what that Italian musical term means and would certainly understand his calling his piece "Legs in a Row."

A nine-year-old girl was learning a song that contained the phrase "I'm not sentimental." She didn't know what "sentimental" meant, but she did know what "a mental" was (the schoolyard slang for a slightly strange child). Thus she sang "I'm not a mental."

A seventh-grade boy when studying northern Europe in geography class, or social studies as it's called these days, said that he knew quite a bit about Norway, "the place with all the Fords."

While reviewing *Don Quixote* the other evening in preparation for a class, I observed a young teenager peering over my shoulder. She didn't see the title, but asked me what it was. I responded and thought she had properly understood. Instead, having no idea what a "Don" was, she thought I was preparing a story about "a donkey named Hotie."

A final example here will suffice. A first-grade boy studying wars in school had no idea what a "revolution" was, but he did know what a "solution" was, and he figured that a war could be a solution of some kind. Thus, when asked what he was studying in school, he replied that he was learning about "World War I and the Solutionary War."

When children move or travel they are also apt to produce new words for their special little vocabularies. A five-year-old loved Mount Rushmore, which she since refers to as "the face." A three-year-old, who's a bit young to be making these kinds of wonderful errors, has two homes: an apartment in New York City and a country home near Albany. During dinner one summer evening, after inviting one of my children to share her "bump bed" (bunk bed), she said that she knew what country she lived in. The name of the country was "Upstate."

Children, then, create language in all situations in which they find themselves. But the areas in which they are really inventive are political and religious. I will suggest a theory to explain this. We live in a seemingly ritual-free culture. There is something ritualistic about going to bed with the Johnny Carson show, awaking at a precise hour to eat a regular breakfast, and catching the punctual car pool for the trek to the office where we ritually work an eight-hour day. However, this is not the ritual of ceremony. This is not the ritual of prayer, secret code language, special costumes and music, or respect for special symbols. We have very little of this in modern American culture.

Where we do have some ritual is in the political and religious areas of our lives. We have political conventions in which normally serious men and women don straw hats, wave banners, sing songs, shout one another down, stay up all night in one caucus or another, and otherwise express the democratic spirit. We have Fourth of July parades in which floats are decorated in red, white, and blue bunting, and the flag is greeted with a salute or a hand on the heart. We have religious services that involve invocations, benedictions, singing, standing up, and sitting down, and kneeling at appropriate times. We have religious fast days and religious holidays in which customs are preserved. Take Christmas for just one example. We put up trees decorated with heirloom baubles, attend candlelight services, dig out the crèche for the hearth, hang the house with holly, light long tapers, and write cards to people we've neither seen nor heard from for a year. And the list could go on.

What's important about all this to our children and to our understanding of their malapropisms in this area is that we either take our rituals so naturally, or we perform them so rarely, that our children don't always understand just what is going on.

William Safire has reported some delightful political malapropisms produced by children. In a recent *New York Times Magazine* column entitled "I Led the Pigeons to the Flag" (meaning "I Pledge Allegiance to the Flag"), he explains that children need to make the sounds they hear fit the sense in their own heads. Thus, the "light from above" in the song "God Bless America" becomes the "light from a bulb."

As Safire continues, "The most saluted man in America is Richard Stans. Legions of schoolchildren daily place their hands over their hearts to pledge alliegiance to the flag and 'to the republic for Richard Stans.' "

Religious malapropisms provide even more fun, especially those that arise around Christian high holidays such as Easter and Christmas. A young boy was singing in a youth choir in his local Lutheran church, busily preparing for an Easter concert. After practice one day, he came home, puzzled, to ask his mother why they were singing such a weird song in church. She, surprised at his remark, said that "Hosanna, Hosanna, the Lord

God is risen" was not a weird song for Easter. "Oh," he said. "I thought we were singing 'Lasagna, lasagna, the good bread is risen.' "

A younger child always makes the same request for her favorite song at Christmas—the "door song," which is, of course, "Oh, Come Let us Adore Him." My own favorite Christmas story is this one: Molly (age five) and Charlie (age three) had received the gift of a crèche, complete with Mary, Joseph, Jesus, and the Wise Men, from their very devout grandmother. The importance of the little sculptures was explained to them, at least partially—or at least partial was their understanding. Molly, however, unwittingly dubbed the Wise Men the "Wise Guys." Her younger brother, noting that one of the Wise Men was holding a silver tray in his hand, remarked, "One of the Wise Guys is bringing Jesus a pizza." Related to this crèche story is yet another one. The kindergarten daughter of an anything but religious mother was making a crèche at school. The child, having had no religious education, only half understood what she was doing and when asked who the baby was she replied, "Round John Virgin."

A final example or two should make this point clear. A young Chicago child knew more about Humboldt Park than about the church and translated "Jesus seeks the humble heart" as "Jesus sneaks through Humboldt Park." A young New York friend of mine couldn't understand the idea of "world without end," which became "whirlwind on end." And of course, according to Safire, the Twenty-third Psalm is reproduced as "Shirley, good Mrs. Murphy will follow me all the days of my life!"

Certainly, this is language creation again, but it does not arise out of a vacuum or without some growing understanding of how language works. There is a principle behind these inventions which is not dissimilar from the way in which we adults invent new words.

If one investigates the history and development of words in the English language, one will discover that adults make the same "mistakes" in correlating sound and sense as children do.

To cite William Safire's ingenious summary again, we all tend to misdivide words.

Many of the words we use today are mistaken divisions of the past: a "napron" in Middle English became an "apron," while an "eke-name" became a "nickname." This phenomenon, Safire says, also accounts for the "millions of children who consider the letter of the alphabet between *k* and *p* to be 'ellemeno,' and the song 'The Londonderry Air' to be oft thought of as 'The London Derrière.' "

Words also change as they pass from culture to culture, or, in the case of the child, from hearing to understanding. An adult example is illustrated by the folk song "Green Grow the Rushes, Ho," based on a Mexican chant about the American "gringoes."

And we all construct malapropisms of one kind or another, make Freudian slips, and distort aphorisms or clichés. Even college students have been heard to say "Don't take me for granite," "There's more than one pigeon on the beach," and "You're running around like a chicken with its leg cut off."

Children, although they are certainly not imitating our accuracy or our errors, are learning the same language principles that we have learned, are learning, or have mislearned.

# 5: The Child's Sense of Dimension and Relationship

As discussed in Chapter 1, the content words in English have two very general qualities. First, they help us *conceptualize* because of their abilities to categorize, to abstract, to be used in a nonliteral or figurative fashion, and so on.

Content words also enable us to express *relationships* between things. There are certain content words in our language that have meaning because of their relationships to other words. We understand that something is hot because we have some notion of what is cold; we understand that one can dine or that one can eat; we understand that one can buy from someone who sells. These pairs, respectively, illustrate certain semantic properties of our language. In the case of "hot" and "cold," we see that English words can relate to one another because they are opposites—or *antonyms*—of one another. In the case of "dine" and "eat," we see that English words relate because they are similar to one another, or *synonyms*. In the case of "buy" and "sell," we see that English words relate because they depend upon one another for full meaning; they are *reciprocals*. Moreover, English words can sound the same, but mean very different things. We may have *read* a *red*-covered book yesterday; this is an example of words that are *homonyms*.

It is not until children are of school age that they even begin to understand these semantic concepts. Their learning of the principle of opposition and reciprocity is dealt with here. Their learning of the principle of synonymity (the basis for many jokes) and homonymy (the basis for most puns) is pursued in Chapter 6, "The Child as Humorist."

## Antonymy and the Child's Sense of Dimension

In general, preschool children are unable to understand the notion that some words indicate, in their very meaning, an opposite quality. The development of this understanding seems to come along with the development of their cognitive skills, and at this stage, young children are denoters; that is, they are interested in talking about the here and now, the observable world, the world that they can touch and feel, and somehow control or play with. At the same time, they are syntactically bound in terms of their understanding of how language works. They are dependent upon word order for meaning. That is, if they hear a word like "shiny," they anticipate that the next appropriate word in the utterance will be the name of something that is "shiny" such as "truck."

If one holds in mind that young children are denoters and are busy learning the word order of English, it will be obvious why young children have real trouble with the English antonym system at the preschool age.

Because they are denoters and interested in understanding the here and now of their observable experience, they learn something about the antonym system. They may have been burned and learn the word "hot"; touching an ice cube to the burn produces the sensation and knowledge of what "cold" means in relationship to "hot." In the summer, they go to bed when it is "dark" and awake when it is "light." These elementary sets of opposites, based on sensual experience, are learned early by the preschool child.

But anything conceptual or abstract is beyond them at this time, for they have little understanding of the abstractability of language. For instance, a seven-year-old girl who was learning opposites in language arts was riding to school with her four-year-old brother. Eager to test him in terms of what she knew, she began asking him to respond to certain words. To "hot" he easily replied "cold"; to "night," "day"; to "dark," "light"; and so on with words that had some referent to the world of sense experience. In an attempt to trick him, she then asked what was the opposite of "on and off, on and off, on and off." What she wanted in reply was "off and on, off and on, off and on." Very perplexed, the young boy thought for a long time and responded, "Stop playing with the TV set," the only thing he could think of that was physically or denotatively related to the "on and off" idea. Preschool children only understand antonymns as those words relate to their everyday physical experience.

Children who are preschoolers are not only bound to the denotative world. They are equally bound to the syntax or grammatical system they have been so diligently learning since birth. They are dependent for a large part of their meaning on the order in which words are uttered. If one gave a "word-association" test to most four-year-olds, the results would give the researchers more insight into the syntactic sense of the four-year-old than into that child's semantic sense. To repeat an earlier example, if one asked a preschooler to respond to "shiny," the child would more than likely respond with the name of something that shines, for the child has a sense that a word like "shiny" functions as an adjective and requires a noun for meaning.

The most difficult of the oppositions in English to learn are those that deal with dimension, those word pairs that express spatial and volume characteristics. Children have an often peculiar and rarely understood sense of the physical dimensions of their world. It is not sufficient merely to note that children, because they are physically little, see the world as populated by giants. It is not just that their perspective is non-adult; their cognition and expression are as well.

Many studies have been made over the past decade in an

attempt to understand the child's acquisition of dimensional concepts of an abstract nature, but none of them are very conclusive. One of the better summaries of those many studies can be found in *Language Acquisition*, by Jill and Peter de Villiers (Harvard University Press, 1978). Part of this chapter is based on their summations of studies too varied and vast to reproduce here.

The relations most often studied, and most often confused by young children, are big and little, tall and short, high and low, long and short, wide and narrow, fat and skinny, thick and thin, and deep and shallow—and the pairs tend to be learned in the order listed.

The earliest pair to appear in child language is big and little, but children have trouble mastering the way in which size is related to the context in which the size word is used. They can see that they are big and their baby brother is little, but as one child was heard saying: "Daddy is big and Max is little. I'm big but Max is little." He paused, apparently trying to fit himself in as the middle person in this measure, and then said, "Dad is big, big." To further illustrate, I refer to an experiment with big and little summarized in *Language Acquisition*. The experimenter, Susan Carey, set up a "let's pretend" tea party to which she invited several four- and five-year-old children and their respective dolls. Into a scene of miniature tables and chairs, minuscule cups and saucers, and tiny dolls, Carey introduced a shot glass. The children sensed that the glass was "little" from their perspective, but when it was placed on the table, they realized that it was "big," out of proportion to their little tea sets. As one girl said, "It's a little glass for me and a big glass for them . . . and a largerger glass for her," as she pointed to the tiniest doll at the table.

Because big and small are learned earliest, they are overused to express all kinds of relational concepts. Things tall, high, long, full, wide, and so on are all "big"; things short, low, skinny, and so on are all "small." A little boy commented that his grandparents couldn't come to a birthday party, not because they weren't children, but because they were "too big."

The other pairs are learned later, and the explanations for the difficulty in their acquisition vary from researcher to researcher. The two most common explanations are these:

1. Pairs such as tall and short, high and low, and long and short refer to more than one semantic dimension or conception and are thus more complex than big and little. Big and little, as we have just seen, can be used to describe any dimension, whether of height, volume, width, or whatever. The later-learned pairs require more conceptual sophistication. For instance, "high" requires one to conceptualize beyond size-in-general (which was good enough for "big") and to add to the idea of size the concept of "vertical." So too with "long," which requires one to go beyond size-in-general by adding the concept of "horizontal." The other pairs, such as wide and narrow, fat and skinny, thick and thin, and deep and shallow, require even more sophisticated a sense of dimension and are way beyond most young children.

2. Pairs such as these have negative and positive poles, and children are more inclined to understand the positive pole than the negative. Thus, they learn one part of the pair to the exclusion of the other. By "positive" is meant a kind of semantic neutrality; by "negative" is meant a kind of semantic judgment or assumption. For example, if one asks how tall a tree is, one is asking for an objective guess about height which implies nothing. If, however, one asks how short a tree is, one is already assuming that the tree is not very tall. The same thing is true with long and short. If one asks how long a table is, one is asking for an objective measurement of the table; if one asks how short a table is, the assumption is that the table is short.

The positive pole in each of these pairs is the one children understand first. Perhaps this is because of some ordering of semantic and conceptual difficulty. To learn "tall," the child must put together what she knows both about "big" and about height. To also add assumption to the conception may be just too difficult. For whatever reason, the positive pole of each pair tends to be applied to both dimensions for some time.

Another set of word pairs which are difficult for children are some and all, and more and less. From the time they are about two years old, children use part of these terms in such statements as "allgone milk" and "more milk," but they use them to comment about the present condition of their milk or to request more milk. They have no sense that those words are also conceptual and can be used *contrastively*. Learning the relationships of these words comes very slowly, and they get confused with earlier learned pairs such as big and little, and tall and short.

Many elementary school children, when they are taught mathematical and measurement concepts, are given a test similar to this: Given an array of various-sized containers filled with liquid—some tall, some big around but short, some flat and long—they are asked to determine which container holds the greatest volume of water. The errors in these kinds of exercises are many, since children tend to opt for the descriptive, relational term with which they are the most comfortable. Hence, in looking for the most liquid (or "bigness"), they tend to look, secondly, for the relationship they learned next (or "tallness"). Thus, no matter which container holds the most water, the tallest container will almost always be selected as the "right" one.

Parents and teachers alike are often frustrated in their attempts to explain this experiment to young children. What they seem to ignore is that children's conceptions are often expressed in the language they have at hand and understand. They simply don't have the semantic vocabulary to express their knowledge fully.

But, once the some and all, more and less concepts are learned, children become adamant about meaning. One boy, at six years of age, was asked if he knew some of the alphabet. He said, "No." The interviewer was perplexed, for the child was nearly a reader at five, and asked again, "Are you sure you don't know some of the alphabet?" This time, the boy said, *"No!* I know *all* of it."

## Reciprocals and Causation

Reciprocals are those content words whose meaning depends upon a relationship that is usually causal. For instance, if something drops, it has been caused to fall; "feed" depends upon being caused to eat; "fill" means to cause to be full; "give" requires that someone take; "buy" requires that someone sell, and so on. Philip Dale in *Language Development* (cited earlier) gives good examples of child errors in trying to understand reciprocity and causation. Children who often drop things, as often say "I (or me) falled the glass," and children get "fulled up" on lunch.

Why these terms are so difficult for children has not been satisfactorily explained. Nor has their strange sense of causation in general, causation that is not based simply on reciprocal terms. My graduate students recorded these comments about how one gets to the moon:

"To get to the moon. Bring some extra pants and bring some underpants and bring a little baby suitcase. I'm gonna be big when I go on the moon. Big moon. We, you go on the big big moon and I go on the little moon. The big, big moon is too big for you." When asked how he was going to get there, the child said, "Dad will drop us off. Dad's gonna go on the big moon, and Mom's gonna go on the big moon. The kids go on the little moon. I'm gonna fly away."

Another child makes Easter eggs like this:

"Just cook em, no boil the eggs. Then you paint em yourself. You put em in shake and bake." Asked if he knew what "shake and bake" was, he replied, "Its a set they show you on TV and then there's a Easter chicken picks up and goes what they are. In the middle they show you how it works. It has hand puppets too. For your hands to play with. It has the sizzling diamonds that you put in and that's to get some color."

A final example of cause and effect or process as understood by a preschooler has to do with the arrival of Santa Claus. According to one young boy, "Santa lands on the roof and comes down the fireplace." If there happens to be a fire going, "He will kill it with a fly swatter or something. Then he'll put it in a box and call some cops or firemen to put it outside."

## Number and Quantity

The spontaneous speech of children, unlike that recorded in the structured experiments referred to earlier, reveals that once a dimension, whether of volume, time, or quantity, gets past the easy-to-measure, easy-to-count stage, accuracy matters not one whit. Bigness becomes infinite, time becomes perpetual, and number becomes incredibly multiple.

The child's sense of time is particularly off-base in terms of adult measures. Although our children know the words for days, weeks, months, and years, what those abstractions mean to them is almost nothing. Following are some of their comments about time:

Andy, five years old, when asked how many days a week he went to school, answered "three weeks." Chad, aged six, had the flu for thirty months and his loose tooth is predicted to come out in six months. Spencer, aged five, will have a birthday in sixty months. Another child was going to go somewhere "in about a hundred seconds."

Numbers confuse children. Once there are more things than the child can conveniently count (say ten or twenty), the actual count becomes meaningless. Justin, five years old, obviously has a favorite numerical symbol for "a great deal." In complaining that his home held too many guests at Christmastime, he said that there were "10,052 people" there; likewise, his *Star Wars* spaceship carries "10,052 people in it." Yet, in the countable world, children can be very accurate. When asked how many miles from school he lived, the child replied, "It ain't no miles. It's four blocks."

The available research on children's acquisition of relational concepts and words to express those concepts is not definitive, but it does seem clear that they have difficulty, even into the early elementary grades, with such expressions. The problem they have with relationships may not be as much linguistic as perceptual. After all, big is supposed to be big-in-general, not necessarily in relationship to something that is small. Reality, for children, may well be in the eye of the beholder and not a linguistic matter at all.

For one reason or another, children finally do catch on to the rudiments of English sounds, structure, and meaning—and then a whole new area of discovery opens up to them. They become *intentionally* and *purposively* aware of the doubleness of language with which this text began. They begin to notice that language can be used in both figurative and literal, connotative and denotative, ways. They learn that language is not merely an instrument of communication through which they can elicit favors and other behaviors, that language is not merely an instrument by which they can communicate feelings, that language is not merely an instrument by which they can demonstrate their knowledge of the tangible world, but that language is a system that can be manipulated for sheer pleasure and humor. They begin, as the next chapter discusses, to discover linguistic ambiguity and its consequence, the making of jokes and/or riddles.

# 6: The Child as Humorist

Earlier in the book, when I was discussing the various qualities of English content words, I noted that English words were often ambiguous, that certain words, phrases, and sentences can mean more than one thing. Often the intended meaning is determined only by the context or the speaker's intonation.

Basically there are three kinds of ambiguity in English, as suggested by Jill and Peter de Villiers' *Language Acquisition,* cited earlier.

First, there is what may be called *lexical ambiguity,* whereby many English words that sound the same mean very different things. This quality of words is called *homonymy* and can be illustrated by a few simple examples.

"Red" and "read" sound the same; yet, the first refers to a color and is a noun or adjective, while the second refers to the act of reading a book sometime in the past and is a verb. In the Midwest, "Mary," "merry," and "marry" sound alike; yet, the first refers to a woman's name and is a proper noun, the second describes a joyful feeling and is an adjective, and the last refers to the act of being wed and is a verb. "Board" and "bored" provide another example. "Board" can refer either to a piece of lumber, or to food eaten on a contractual basis, as in "paying for board and room at college." On the other hand, "bored" describes a condition of disinterest, or refers to the past-tense action of drilling a hole. "Stick" can refer to something as general as any polelike object made of wood or something as specific as a hockey stick; it can also be used as a verb to describe the act of putting something in place with a kind of adhesive, and with some variation of word ending, could be used as an adjective ("sticky") to describe the condition of a thing. In this last case "stick" is not an example of a homonym, but of a word that has a variety of meanings although the spelling remains the same.

The second and third kinds of ambiguity arise from the structure of our language. To explain, Noam Chomsky, a modern theorist concerned with how English works as a system by which we all communicate, posits that English has two levels. It has a *surface structure* which is the way we actually use language. The way each of us puts words together to form our own sentences that are uttered in our own regional or social dialect constitutes our use of the surface of language. This leads to a kind of ambiguity which, for want of a better term, can be called *surface structure ambiguity*. This ambiguity arises because of the groupings or relationships of various words in the sentence. For example, the meaning of the phrase "skinny boys and girls" is unclear. Does it mean that both the boys and the girls are skinny? Or that only the boys are skinny?

We also have a *deep structure* in our language which depends upon rules of English that we rarely bring to consciousness. We just know that there is something wrong with the expression "the bachelor's wife" and "The green Chicago is running." We just know that, although the phrase and sentence are put together in the right way, they simply don't make any sense. Likewise, we know that a sentence such as "Bird the fly black" is somehow not right, even though we know the meaning of each individual word. What the deep structure provides us with are those rules by which we determine whether or not an English sentence is semantically sensible and/or grammatical—and this intrinsic knowledge we share in common as members of the same speech community.

Nonetheless, the rules of the deep structure which we have all learned and internalized are not always clear on the surface, not always clear in our actual expression. Thus, the third kind of ambiguity is formed, and is illustrated by the following sentences:

"The eating of the chicken was sloppy" could mean either that the chicken was a sloppy eater or that the people who were eating the chicken were themselves sloppy. One would have to uncover the rules of sentence formation in order to have a clear meaning. For example, did the speaker develop this sentence out of the basic idea that the *chicken* was eating or that *people* were eating? The same kind of ambiguity is found in a sentence used earlier. "She enjoyed boring old ladies" could mean that she enjoyed old ladies who were boring or that she enjoyed being boring in the presence of old ladies.

It has been argued by some that the child's recognition of these kinds of ambiguity is developmental, that children first discover lexical ambiguity and recognize that words that sound the same can mean different things, that they then learn surface structure ambiguity and realize that the combinations of certain words in a sentence can affect meaning, and that they finally learn deep structure ambiguity and realize that the relationship of the subject to the whole corpus of English meaning and word-order rules can produce interesting utterances. Other studies dispute the claim and argue that all are recognized at about the same time, during the early years of elementary school.

Whatever is the truth about the order of acquisition—and that we don't know the truth indicates how much we have yet to learn about the acquisition of meaning in children—children do somehow come to the understanding that word meanings are not always precise and solitary, that words provide us with ways to assess alternatively the environment and our experience, and, most important for this chapter, that words have a quality that allows them to be played with, to be manipulated, to be fun and inventive. Because of this ambiguity in language, children are able to make jokes and riddles.

Because children become aware of the ambiguity of language,

they can manipulate that quality to their own delight, and the delight—or dismay—of their parents. In earlier chapters, funny things that children said were recounted, but those funny remarks were accidental. They were malapropisms that arose when the children were trying to understand an adult concept in childish terms. The examples of child humor that follow in this chapter are *intentional*. The inventors of the jokes, riddles, and puns knew just what they were doing. But one must keep in mind that these inventions did not occur at just any age. Unless a four-year-old is very sophisticated in the use of language, intentional humor will not work for her audience. A typical four-year-old joke would be something like this: "Why did the apple cross the road? To get the banana." She will shriek with laughter while her audience, if adult, will moan in despair. The point is that intentional humor starts as a grade school phenomenon.

Just as there are three kinds of ambiguity in English, there are three levels of joke-telling. The first level is the most commonly heard in first through third grade, and the humor depends upon the child's recognition of what has been called lexical ambiguity. The child comes to understand that words have a literal meaning (for example, "bat" literally means a flying night creature) and that they have a more fanciful or figurative meaning (for example, one can "bat" away the cobwebs). They learn that words that sound the same, homonyms, can refer to very different things. The source of humor comes about when the child realizes that the literal meaning of a word can provoke his audience to laugh. The child intentionally "misunderstands" the figurative side of meaning and responds literally.

A child was listening to an explanation of the building of a beamed two-story ceiling. The adult was trying to describe how the workmen were able to reach the high ceiling and position the beams. That they used "scaffolding" was beyond her; "a kind of ladder" didn't do. When told that the supports were pipes that were iron, she gave up her curiosity about the ceiling and picked up on "iron." She giggled and said, "We can't iron the ceiling." When the adult said she didn't mean that kind of iron, the child said, "Let's not talk about that." Enough was enough.

A child whose parents are fond of imbibing sherry after school answered a telephone call for his father, the professor. The caller was a student whose name happened to be Sherri. This amused the young man, who, making a grand joke, said that his father was talking to a wine bottle.

This first level of joke-making makes for frustrating conversations between a parent and a child. The parent asks the child to pick up his room. The child responds, "I can't. It's too heavy." Or the parent asks the child if she can "tell me what time it is." The child responds, "Yes." Or the parent tells the child to "get on your boots" and the child sits on them. Or the parent, encouraging a young musician, says, "Let's jump into the next song," and the child puts a piece of sheet music on the floor and jumps on it. This is the level at which the young musician, who has just learned a piece written by Handel, remarks that he didn't know that "a handle could write music."

All of these are examples of intentional humor based on the literal meaning of words that have a possibility of multiple meaning. They are based on the simplest recognition of ambiguity. "Iron" and its multiple meanings (the object used to get wrinkles out of cotton shirts and a kind of metal) set off the first story. "Sherry" set off the ambiguity of proper name and a kind of wine in the second. "Pick up," meaning to clean up and to lift up, prompted the next; "can" and its confusion with "will you," the next; "get on," meaning both to put on and to sit or stand on, the next; "jump into," meaning both to move quickly into and to actually enter in a physical way, the next; and so on.

Really creative joke-telling begins with the recognition of the second kind of ambiguity—surface structure ambiguity—a recognition that signals level two in joke-telling and riddle-making. At this level, children intentionally seek out sentence structures in which homonyms hover. Unlike level one, in which humor is produced by the intentional emphasis of literal meaning to the exclusion of the intended and more figurative meaning, level two is characterized by the rejection of literal meaning and the elaboration, instead, of the more figurative possibilities. This is the level of the pun.

It is at this level that one might hear jokes and riddles of this kind:

> Why can you never starve in the desert?
> Because of the sand which is there.

Or:

> A termite wandered into a bar and asked, "Is the bartender here?"

This kind of humor also arises from informal conversation. A mother had been explaining to her seven-year-old son what B.C. and A.D. mean. The boy understood, apparently, that A.D. certainly had something to do with "after," for when told one evening to get his pajamas on, he replied that he would "A.D.," meaning "After *Dukes*" (*of Hazard* on TV). The same child's younger brother was injured in a fall and the mother tried to explain that they must be very careful how Max was handled, "for he has to heal." To this the older boy said, "Yes, and he has two arms, two legs, two hands," and so on.

All of these examples of intentional humor are based on the rejection of the literal meaning of words, and the recognition that words are ambiguous. The homonym "sandwiches" was substituted for the literal "sand which is" in the first story; the homonym "bartender" was substituted for the literal "bar tender" meaning soft wood in the second; the homonym "heal" meaning heel of the foot was substituted for the literal "heal" meaning get well in the last.

Finally, older children become even more sophisticated in their riddle-making and joke-making, for they come to recognize the third kind of ambiguity of English, the ambiguity that is produced by the deep structure of the language. They come to understand that certain kinds of nouns or sentence subjects are semantically restricted, that to break the rules will produce an utterance that is not sensible. Thus, they know that "the bachelor's wife" and "The green Chicago are running" are wrong because there is a semantic rule in the word "bachelor" that precludes having a wife, and a city can neither be green nor run. Knowing these deep structure rules, they can then bend them and produce humor at level three.

A typical joke at this level would delight a ten-year-old.

> "I can jump higher than the Empire State Building."
> "How come?"
> "Because the Empire State Building can't jump!"

Age obviously has a great deal to do with the ability of a child to recognize humor and ambiguity at this level, for Jill and Peter de Villiers write about their experience in telling this joke to a four-year-old. The child destroyed it in trying to repeat it to a friend: "Hey! Guess what! The Empire State Building can't jump as high as I can!"

This chapter has discussed jokes and riddles that children make up for their own delight, the delight of other children, and the delight or dismay of their parents, teachers, and other adults. Of course, children's senses of stories worth telling are not limited to jokes, riddles, puns, and other one-liners. They are also increasingly interested in the humor, pathos, excitement, vicarious experiences, and adventures offered to them in the stories that others tell them. They are storytellers themselves. Children returning from camp are eager to explain about the climactic canoe trip; children returning from grandparents' homes are eager to recall the rides at the amusement park; children home from school simply want to relate the day's playground scenario. Children also love to gossip and pass on tales about one another.

But aside from storytelling, they like to be told and read stories, and the readers among them like to read stories themselves. Part III addresses the subject of children and stories, in the simplest sense. In a wider sense it addresses children's reactions to stories, some of which are also literature. It also provides parents, teachers, and others with suggestions on books for reading to children and having children read.

# PART III: *On Reading and Writing*

# 7: The Language of Narration: The Younger Child

As children mature, they learn about the meaning of the words in the language they are acquiring at home and school and among their peers. There remains another vast source from which children learn how language "means," however, that has not yet been considered. This source is the stories they read, hear, or tell, or watch on television or in the theater. As parents, we read stories to our children or buy them books for birthdays and Christmas. We take them to plays at the local college or high school or professional theater. And after carefully selecting the books and the plays for their consumption, we often wonder what they are getting out of all of this. What do these things mean?

The acquisition of meaning seems to be developmental. In large part it is age-dependent. So too is what children get out of what they read and see. What they get out of stories has a great deal to do with their ability to distinguish real from pretend (e.g., people speaking from bears speaking) and psychologically real from simply realistic (e.g., characters with identifiable problems from stories that seem realistic in terms of detail, but that deal with issues not often encountered in the child's experience). Children don't mind if bears talk if the message of their speech is something with which they can identify. On the other hand, they will reject stories that seem realistic if the problems the characters face have little to do with their own emotional lives.

Children appear to go through three distinct stages in their understanding of narrative, and these stages are very closely re-

lated to their linguistic and cognitive development. My studies
suggest that young children, around three years of age, are linguistically busy learning the basic rules of English. Their sense
of meaning is syntactic, as discussed earlier. Thus, a story that is
filled with wonderful words that sound like nouns followed by
words that sound like verbs and preceded by words that sound
like adjectives is accepted enthusiastically. The child is not
content-oriented as much as grammatically attuned. When the
young child does pay attention to content, and she often does,
the lines between the actually real and the pretend do not seem
to matter. The child's cognitive concerns at this age are still
rather primitive. The child is egocentric and concerned with
personal feelings and perceptions—feelings of love, joy, fear, anger, jealousy, and isolation in large part.

Young school-age children, on the other hand, are beginning
to grasp the complex nature of content words and the variety of
interpretation such words make possible. They are beginning to
understand the differences between literal and figurative meaning, and, consequently, between real and pretend stories. Moreover, they are becoming more socialized than the preschoolers
and tend to be more interpretive, caring at this stage about what
characters feel, think, and do. Entering a more adult world, they
encounter narrative experiences that they don't quite understand, and they try to accommodate those new experiences to
those they do understand, much as they accommodated new
words to sound patterns.

Just as the child who hears "I pledge allegiance to the flag"
readjusts what he hears to what he understands ("I led the
pigeons to the flag"), so does the child reader. As Kenneth
Goodman and others point out in various studies of what has
been called "miscuing" (see Yetta and Kenneth Goodman, *Miscue Analysis: Applications to Reading Instruction,* National Council of
Teachers of English), children, when reading narratives, often
come across situations that are not common to them, situations
they've never experienced. Thus, when they encounter new

words that refer to these uncommon situations, they substitute a more familiar word to adjust the content to their own experience.

For example, in a miscue study a young girl was reading a story about a woodsman and his wife. Because it was set in another place and time, some of the things in the story—particularly the notion that the man worked at or near home and that the family made its own butter—didn't sit right with her and she made the following changes;

| | |
|---|---|
| *Text:* | If you *stay home* to do my work, you'll have to *make butter.* |
| *Child:* | If you *start home* (as from work), you'll have to *make bread* (a more usual household activity). |

Later in the text the big pig bumps into a churn, a word for which the child substituted "cream."

Apparently the child did not have any particular trouble decoding the missed words. She had trouble understanding what they could possibly have to do with a family situation and family chores.

Finally, older children, those in the upper elementary grades, develop a new narrative sense. They not only distinguish between real and pretend, but between stories and plays that are psychologically real, i.e., of real interest to them, and those that are "just school." This will be discussed at length, as these three stages are considered by example.

## The Preschool Child

Preschool children have yet to learn that words are ordered in a certain way in English, that words have little endings that change their meaning, and that the rules for both cannot be broken without resultant confusion. Young children hang on the order of words for meaning and are equally delighted with either of these expressions:

> The running elephants stormed the forest.
> The ticking elephants rode the elevator.

Neither statement makes much semantic sense to the young child, but the words are all in order and sound wonderful. This syntactical dependence of the young child helps to explain his delight at Dr. Seuss stories. They all sound so wonderful, even though the child does not begin to try to conceptualize the reality of green eggs and ham. This, in part, also explains their early love of poetry or nursery rhymes. The sounds of the language are far more important than the meaning being conveyed. Children have no desire or need to know the political background of "Humpty Dumpty." They simply love the sound of the verse.

To a great extent, then, young children love stories because of the way they sound. Any meaning that they get from early tales is language-related. Yet, preschoolers also have some sense of content, as revealed by the stories they ask to have reread, the stories they tell, and their reactions to visual enactments of stories.

Favorite stories of preschoolers seem to be fairy tales and tales in which animals take on human characteristics. Both kinds of narrative deal with basic, human emotions by removing them from realistic contexts. They involve the child's emotions without seeming too actual and threatening, for children seem to seek in stories some acceptance of their own confusion, fears, and frustrations.

In *The Uses of Enchantment* (Knopf, 1976), Bruno Bettelheim makes a strong argument for the importance of fairy tales in the young child's learning and reading experience. He argues that fairy tales operate on at least two levels. On one level, they are simply exciting tales. The poor stepsister goes to the ball and wins the handsome prince after all. The lovely girl's wicked stepmother condemns her to a life with dwarfs. The princess must beg the murderous king for her life. A girl encounters a wolf on the way to her grandmother's house.

On the second level, fairy tales reach into the psyche of the young child through hidden, psychological, universal messages. "Cinderella" addresses feelings of spite and meanness while nonetheless rewarding independent virtue. "Snow White" addresses envy of one generation for another, particularly of mother and daughter, and sets the child in a world of little people over which she has control. Scheherazade does not simply fall in love with the murderous king, or beg for her life. Instead, Scheherazade and the king can be seen as representing warring forces within the psyche, i.e., the depressed and destructive versus the good and the reasonable. The peace between Scheherazade and the king suggests that we can be whole, that the psyche's two sides can compromise. "Little Red Riding Hood" deals with threat of a sexual nature, and the saving of the child.

The choice among various tellings of the fairy tales is not simply between illustrators, as many parents think. The content of the fairy tales also varies from book to book, with one extreme being represented by editions close to the original Grimm Brothers stories and the other by the Walt Disney Golden Books series.

In the Grimm manner, the stories are more violent, more passionate, perhaps even more frightening. Cinderella, for instance, not only lives happily ever after, but the birds pluck out her stepsister's eyes. Goldilocks is not merely reprimanded by the bears, but leaps out the window and breaks her neck. In the Disney stories, the endings are sweeter and the psychological message in part forgone for a moral lesson instead. The central point of fairy tales, however, has little to do with whether they conclude with a catastrophe or happy endings. What matters more is that they feature passive protagonists who are acted upon, largely because children who listen to them feel at the mercy of events and want to be reassured.

According to an article in *Time* magazine (July 20, 1981), "The real business of fairy tales is not propaganda. It is to help the young deal with anger, sibling rivalry, fear of separation and death, and the eerie omnipotence of the adult world." The same could be said for all decent, strong, children's literature. As Bruno Bettelheim argues, "The fairy tale offers solutions in ways that the child can grasp on his level of understanding."

When a group of young children were asked to recount their favorite stories, the most popular were "Cinderella," "Goldilocks," "The Three Little Pigs," and *The Wizard of Oz* among others. The recountings reveal the children's concerns about adult behavior toward children, cruelty, evil, retribution, and family relationships. For example, Cinderella had to sweep and wash all the floors. Her work finished, Cinderella dressed to go to the dance and "the girls broke her dress. Rip, rip, rip." Cinderella finally "got the dress" and "with her magic wand she met somebody. They danced and danced." Cinderella loses her shoe and it is later tried on by various people. It fits Cinderella and "them two got mad. They never did know. The end."

Similar concerns for naughty behavior show up in the recounting of "Goldilocks." Very few children err in the telling of the tale, for it is, in its very nature, repetitive, but the ending varies from teller to teller. The extremes run from those children who know the original ending—that Goldilocks broke her neck jumping out the window—to the more modest "Goldilocks jumped out the window and she never came in somebody's house when they weren't home," to a real attempt to justify Goldilocks' behavior in this sample in which Papa Bear says, "The next time the door is locked she better mind her manners." And Baby Bear says, "I hope she comes back sometime. She seemed so nice."

The "Three Little Pigs" moral is lost on all the preschoolers researched for this study. The "build a firm foundation" motif mattered not a bit to the children, who were fascinated by the demise of the wolf; some of them had the wolf falling into boiling water, but most of them had him "broiled to nothing," a means of cooking with which the children were apparently more familiar.

A cinematic favorite of many children is *The Wizard of Oz.* The children are most assuredly frightened of the wicked witch, even though some of them know at some intellectual level (although not emotional) that she's not real. Two things seem to delight the children: that everyone gets his wish ("the wizard gave the scarecrow a brain, then he gave the tin man a heart, then he gave the lion a drop of courage. That's all. The end"), and that the witch gets her due ("Dorothy melted the witch. Yep. She put a pan of water on her. Dorothy said, 'I'm so sorry,' but the others said '*All right,* Dorothy!' ").

Stories that feature animals with human characteristics also enchant preschoolers, whose favorites tend to be the *Babar* stories, and the *Little Bear* stories by Else Minarik. And here again, the children are intrigued by the adventures of Babar, in the first instance, and their identification with the feelings of the animals in both cases. The language of these stories is patterned in simple English form, with nothing much more complicated than a noun, a verb, and an adverb or location. The children can feel comfortable within that linguistic context while they begin to unravel meaning. *A Kiss for Little Bear,* for instance, is about "happiness and angriness" that result from "things getting all mixed up."

We have seen that preschool children gain two kinds of meaning from what they read and hear and see. First, they are taught by books and movies and plays that English means something simply because of the way the words are put together in any given expression. Second, they are learning that narratives mean something personal and that stories can make them feel less isolated in their own feelings of anger, rivalry, cruelty, and wishes for retribution. Narratives not only give our children an added impetus to understand the working of language; they also provide them with a means to understand themselves.

## The Young School-Age Child

Young elementary school children (kindergarten through third grade, perhaps) have entered a linguistic world far beyond that of the preschooler. The six- and seven-year-old child has acquired a sense of the importance of English content words and of their qualities of abstraction, ambiguity, metaphor, and the like. This child can make up jokes, riddles, and puns, and can begin to interpret seriously, in a meaningful way, the narratives that he encounters. Of special concern to the young elementary child is the separation of real from pretend. This child wants to know—and wants others to know—that she or he is not easily fooled, that pretend is pretend and real is real. But making this distinction is not always easy, especially in response to visual narratives, such as those on television or the stage.

Typical questions at this age are: Is that man really jumping off the cliff or pretending to? Is that really happening or is that a camera trick? Is that soldier really dead or is that an actor pretending he's hurt? Are those really trained elephants or are they people in costumes? Are those real lords fighting a real duel (in *Romeo and Juliet*) or is that just pretend?

Because young school-age children are moving out of a narrative world that is full of rhyme, nonsense, fantasy, fairy tale, and personification, they tend at this age to prefer realistic narratives, ones that address either their sense of adventure or their emotional natures. Two or three examples will illustrate this point.

One of my seven-year-old's favorite books is *The Black Stallion,* by Walter Farley (Random House, 1977)—favorite both because of its realism and adventure and because it was filmed and thus became visually alive for him. As my child related the story to me: "First the ship sank and the black horse swims. The boy grabs the rope and he's alive, and he stays there on a desert island for fifty months. Then a ship comes along and says, 'Where did that ship go?' 'Oh, right on this desert island it sank.'

'How did you get there?' 'That great big black horse saved me.' 'Oh, that's it.' "

As implied by the *Black Stallion* example, children in the early elementary grades enjoy narratives that are about animals, but the animal stories to which they are drawn now depict the animals as subject, hero, or helpmate. The animals no longer speak. The animals become brave and protective, but they are clearly not personifications of human beings. Favorite animal stories in our home are the many novels by Jim Kjelgaard such as *Stormy,* and *Irish Red* (Bantam Skylark, 1981). In addition to narratives about animals, documentary discussions of animals intrigue children of this age. The National Geographic Society publications are illustrated with color photographs and have an easy-to-read text.

As noted, adventure stories, too, are favorites of the young (and older) reader. In 1981, Bantam Books put out a series of books called *Choose Your Own Adventure.* As teasers that get children to read, they work. Each adventure, with titles such as *The Lost Jewels of Nabooti,* begins with a kind of introduction and exposition; then, every few pages or so, the reader is asked if he'd like the adventure to continue in a cave, on a ship, or whatever. The reader selects the next element of the adventure by picking up the story on the given page and reading until the next choice. The result is as many as forty possible conclusions to any given tale, and readers seem to delight in this choice.

Young readers do not, however, choose only to read realistic fiction dealing, as often as not, with animals, nor do they read only adventure stories. They turn also to books more reminiscent of their early reading, to books that fantasize, retell fairy and folk tales, or feature animal characters. They seem to turn to these books because they tend to address more than the child's need for authenticity and excitement; they address, as they did before, his emotional needs. Elementary school children often feel estranged, a little odd or "out of it," sometimes defiant. They have recently entered school, made the initial separation from their parents which seems a bit like abandonment, and moved into a peer-dominated environment where acceptance does not come automatically for the first time. They make mistakes in a public world in public view, and some of the traditional narratives can give them insight and help them understand their new fears and feelings.

Although the examples used here are not necessarily examples of the best books for young readers, they are favorites of children of my acquaintance. Consider, as a retold folk tale, Tomie de Paola's *The Clown of God* (Scholastic Books, 1978) and many other books of his, and Leo Lionni's *Frederick* (Pinwheel Books, Knopf, 1973). These books deal with life cycles, talents, individuality, and rejection and acceptance in very different ways. They are written in language the child can understand. Although the prose style goes beyond the simple noun/verb/object or location pattern that the four- and five-year-old is just getting comfortable with, the style is not beyond the six-to-nine-year-old. The sentences combine phrases, but not in any complicated way, and the vocabulary, although rich, is not beyond an early reader.

*The Clown of God* is about an orphaned boy with no food or good clothes, who was nonetheless happy because he could do something wonderful—he could juggle. He juggled in the marketplace in exchange for soup until a troupe of traveling players let him join them. He became more and more famous juggling the rainbow of colors that concluded with the juggling of the gold ball, the "sun of heavens." Finally, famous, he was able to travel and entertain on his own. One day, en route to an engagement, he came upon two Franciscan brothers with whom he shared his plentiful food; they shared with him the wisdom of St. Francis that "if you give happiness to people, you give glory to God as well." But the years passed, the boy became old, times became hard, and he began to drop the golden ball. Fleeing for his life, he gave up juggling forever, returning to the abject poverty from which he had begun. He decided to go home, making it as far as the local monastery, the home of the Franciscans. He, now a weary old man, entered the church on the evening of the procession of gifts. The church emptied, and he approached the statue of the Lady and the Child.

"The Child in the Lady's arms seemed so serious, so stern," that the old juggler decided to make him smile. He juggled and juggled, performing the rainbow and causing the sun of heaven to soar. He had never juggled so well. Exclaiming "for you, sweet child, for you," the old man fell dead to the ground, but "the child was smiling and in his hand he held the golden ball."

*Frederick* is about a seemingly lazy field mouse. "Since winter was not far off, the little mice began to gather corn and nuts and wheat and straw. They all worked day and night. All—except Frederick." His answer to their continual nagging and questioning was that he was working. "I gather sun rays for the cold dark winter days. I gather colors for the winter is gray." Winter did come, and the mice sought their prepared refuge. All was well for a while, but soon the food was gone, the cold penetrated, and they had run out of things to say. Then they remembered what Frederick had said. " 'What about your supplies, Frederick?' they asked." He told them about sun rays, and "when he told them of the blue periwinkles, and red poppies in the yellow wheat, and the green leaves of the berry bush, they saw the colors as clearly as if they had been painted in their minds." At the conclusion the mice called Frederick a poet, and he responded, "I know it."

Through these examples one can sense, at least, the relationship of children's narratives and their linguistic and cognitive development. Stories that introduce new vocabulary and metaphor within sentence structures the young child can untangle while at the same time fulfilling his desire for vicarious adventure, or information, and reassurance about his differences will always be sought after.

While reading, young elementary school children continue to acquire the meanings that permeate their language, and they come to an increased understanding that a corpus of language, what many of us call literature, can increase their sense of the meaning of their own experience.

Many of us, whether parents and teachers of children or not, have held an idyllic view of childhood, the view reflected in Norman Rockwell paintings of freckle-faced children holding fishing rods, washing the family dog, building a fort in the hot sun, relishing the cotton candy and clowns at the visiting circus, or all spruced-up for the first day of school. The family album probably includes parallel photographs, for we tend to commemorate those events that fulfill our expectations of what life should be all about. We photograph our sons going on their first overnight fishing trip, all asmile, not their terror when the first raccoon they've ever seen sneaks into camp and makes noises in the night. We photograph the water-drenched dog bathers, not the crying child who has just been scratched by an unfriendly dog. We photograph Susie taking Sally by the hand for her first day at kindergarten, not Sally running home during her first recess because school has made her homesick and frightened.

Most of this book has dealt with the clever things children say, with their constant invention, with their lighthearted explanation of what things and actions mean to them. Their response to narratives, though, reminds us that there is a dimension to childhood experience that many of us have forgotten, a dimension that is filled with doubt and fear and envy that becomes apparent when one really listens to children and pays attention to the verbal environment in which they surround themselves, the narrative environment from which they gain additional "meaning."

# 8: The Language of Narration: The Older Child

Talking about school reading texts, one fifth-grade girl commented that "they have no character"; another, that "they're boring." When asked to compare their favorite novels (and Judy Blume novels ranked high for the whole group) to their school assignments, several fifth-graders said that Judy Blume novels are "about real stuff," whereas school books are "just school books." School reading books were not brought home for fun or for leisure reading; library books were.

Upper elementary children are deeply concerned with the difference between school reading texts and the narratives they choose to read on their own, a difference that has something to do with the assumed realism of the first and the psychological reality of the second.

For one reason or another, these children come to a fairly sophisticated sense of "meaning." They can sense, if not articulate, that narratives are meaning*ful* to them or not. This sense of *meaningfulness* is examined in this chapter.

General though these fifth-graders' statements were, I became interested in finding out just what they meant. Determined to find out what children were being asked to read in an attempt to distinguish what they had to read from what they chose to read, I skimmed through most of the textbooks published by the twelve major textbook publishing companies. Finally, I focused my attention on the reading textbooks aimed at the fifth-grade child, published by four major publishing companies.

My first glimpses of those textbooks startled me, delighted

me, and caused me to question the girls' vague comments. Gone were Dick and Jane and Baby Sally. Instead, the texts were peopled by children of all colors named Santiago, Chin Lee, and Mary Whitefeather. Gone were Mommy in her apron and Daddy with his briefcase. Instead, some fathers worked at night in a factory and mothers had jobs outside the home. The content looked like "real stuff" to me, for something revolutionary had obviously happened in the schoolbook industry.

In the early 1970s a revolution did take place in American culture. Protests against the Dick and Jane, middle-class, sexist, white American family image which dominated elementary school textbooks began, grew louder, gained credibility, and reputedly transformed the content of American school books. To be corrected, in particular, was sexist and racist stereotyping.

An early protest against sexism in literature came from the National Organization of Women in Princeton, who, after studying 134 readers from twelve different publishers, could find no acceptable series. An early respondent to the protest was Scott Foresman, the publisher of the Dick and Jane books, which, in 1972, published a guideline entitled *Improving the Image of Women in Textbooks*. This guideline urged writers and editors to avoid such things as sexist language ("when man invented the wheel"), language that demeaned women ("the ancient Egyptians allowed women considerable control over property"), a patronizing tone of voice ("the candidates were B. K. Wilson, President of American Electronic, and Florence Greenwood, a pert, blond grandmother of five"), and role and occupational stereotyping. Other publishers, such as McGraw-Hill, Houghton Mifflin, and Ginn, soon followed Scott Foresman's lead. Demands that racial stereotyping be removed were also made. It was somehow assumed that the reduction and elimination of sex-role and race-role stereotyping would rid elementary school reading books of unexamined cultural assumptions.

A closer look at the new textbooks, however, nullified my delight and my surprise and made the 1970s revolution seem pale. Although the reading books now *look* different, with racially and sexually balanced illustrations, and although they now *sound* different, with children named Chin Lee instead of Dick, the underlying cultural assumptions are still those with which we grew up and those promulgated through the mass media every day. What Francis Fitzgerald has written about the content of American history textbooks in *America Revisted* (Little, Brown, 1980) can be said, as well, of elementary reading texts: "Books portray the world as a utopia of the eternal present—a place without conflict, without malice or stupidity, where Dick (black or white) comes home with a smiling Jane to a nice house in the suburbs."

The image of society presented in even the revolutionized textbooks seems to be this: American children live within cozy, middle-class families where problems are solved in the kitchen over corn flakes. Judging from the textbooks, everything works out in the end. The successful resolution of difficulties rarely has anything to do with conscious effort, nor is anyone ever responsible for the problem itself. According to these books, events happen to people and resolutions settle down on people, but no one does much that is very good or very evil or very thoughtful or very stupid. They live in a world where everyone is pretty much alike, where controversy and struggle do not exist, and where criticism is not encouraged.

This seems to be what the fifth-graders meant when they said that reading textbooks have no "character," that they are "boring" and don't deal with "real stuff." Although textbooks look current in their appreciation of cultural, ethnic, and sexual differences, the stories themselves suffer from sameness, interchangeability of character, and inoffensiveness. In an attempt to reach the average child, textbooks miss most actual children. Textbooks are, in a special sense, untrue, because they speak for a social and economic ideal and do not speak to the psychological needs of the individual child. I will grant that any book might be used to teach a child reading skills and thus serve his or her educational needs. However, it is my argument that books which do not serve a child's psychological needs as well (for example, by giving the child someone with whom to identify, by making the child feel less guilty or isolated) actually discourage the child from reading. A discouraged child will not establish the habit of reading nor feel the lure of a printed story. A discouraged child is far more likely to turn to more effortless and viable options for his leisure, and books have never had such intense competition for the child's leisure time.

Some parents may respond, "So what? Textbooks have never done more than this. I don't care what the books are about as long as my kids are learning to read!" My answer to this remark is threefold and, I think, crucial, because the child who accepts the reality of these stories may then reject his own experience; the child who does accept the reality of his own experience may reject the school books—perhaps even school itself; and the child who is simply disinterested in the stories will not be lured on to read.

First, to cite Francis Fitzgerald, "These bland fictions, propagated for the purpose of creating good citizens, may actually achieve the opposite . . . they may well make young people feel that their own experience of conflict or suffering is unique and perhaps un-American." These fictions may well make children feel bad about their own experience. The child who accepts the bland fictions of textbooks as the norm may well feel guilty about divorced parents and bologna-sandwich lunches when the textbook dads save the day and the textbook moms serve steaming casseroles. Children feel bad about themselves when they are *really* isolated and friendless and read how everything works out for the textbook characters.

Second, some children who trust their own experience with real grief, jealousy, and joy ignore their textbooks and become cynical about school, which becomes "just school," having little to do with the world as they know it.

Third, and most important, the child who neither accepts nor rejects the message of the reading textbook but merely becomes disinterested in reading poses the real problem. Learning to read and wanting to read are two different things. A turned-off child will not develop the habit of reading. He will not feel the lure of a story, and will fill his leisure exclusively with other activities, some very profitable, such as clubs and scouts, weekend athletics, music lessons, and others, like television watching, less so.

Yet, many children do choose to read. Some of their choices may seem like junk to parents, but comic books, TV gossip sheets, romances, horror stories, and joke and riddle books are as popular today as they were when we were children. Some childrens' choices push them way beyond their skills level. Most of their choices involve stories that come alive for them, that challenge them, that encourage criticism, that are even a little naughty. As Alison Lurie recently wrote in the *Times Literary Supplement* (March 1980), memorable children's books have always been at least slightly subversive: "They express feelings not generally approved of or even recognized by grown-ups; they make fun of honored figures and piously held beliefs." Consider Tom Sawyer, who lies and takes a beating for love of Becky Thatcher and who breaks rule after rule in Aunt Polly's household. Consider Huckleberry Finn, who manipulates, wheels, and deals his way down the Mississippi River. Consider Jo, who dares to be a tomboy and take authority for the "little women." Even Nancy Drew is a bright girl who acts on her own initiative and doesn't listen to her father's—or anyone else's—warnings.

Our children choose books to read today—whether Judy Blume novels which agonize over bras and periods, or tales of gourmet giants who consume boy soup—not because the language is at their level or because the content celebrates the same bland values which bombard them from the television set. Instead, they choose to read what is true for them and makes them sad or frightened or giggly or relieved. They choose books which reach them on an emotional and intellectual plane. What they choose to read are not textbook readers but honest literature.

Children's literature has both content and form. Books can have a narrative, a plot, and a set of speaking characters who reveal to children psychological truths. They can reach children's own experience and make them feel normal for feelings of anger and envy, make them feel proud for feelings of compassion and generosity, make them feel less solitary for feelings of abandonment, make them realize that daydreams and fantasies are the order of many of our days. Unlike reading textbooks which too frequently utter platitudes that encourage children to ignore the reality of their own experience or to undervalue it, good children's literature has content that is realistic in the sense of emotional and intellectual honesty, not in the naturalistic sense of showing the shabby and unpleasant aspects of living.

Children's literature also presents itself in various forms and styles. Children's books depend upon vocabulary, sentence forms, and illustrations that are gauged to reach a young reader. These forms, however, are not incorporated for the sole purpose of inculcating skills in the reader. Instead, the style of a children's book is dependent upon the story to be told and the linguistic maturity of the child. For instance, children younger than eight years of age have trouble producing complex sentences, using the helping verb system, and keeping the strong ("sing, sang, sung") and weak ("walk, walked, walked") verbs straight. Thus, children's books aimed at the young reader may avoid those complications of style and find ways to express ideas in simpler format.

A quick look at some readily available books for older children who can handle ambiguity, relational concepts, and figurative language and that meet the criteria of literature, written at various linguistic levels, should dramatize the contrast between those books our children choose to read and those foisted upon them by well-meaning teachers and publishers who have, for too long, assumed that the neutral, the inoffensive, and the culturally normal was the best fodder for children.

Comments such as "In the beginning it was joyous," "It was romantic," "It made me cry," "I loved it," and "Why do people do those things?" were recently overheard while some twelve-year-olds discussed *The Diary of Anne Frank*. Granted, this is pretty heavy stuff for children, but the girls loved the book. They admired the intimacy of the language, and many of them are now being more careful and thoughtful in writing their own diaries. They liked the love interest, an interest that comes earlier to children than it used to. They were tormented by the ways Jews were treated during World War II.

How different is this from the textbook reader which contains a story of a young girl who is supposed to participate in a school pageant whose theme is the "contributions of our ancestors." She can find no one famous in her background to celebrate, but is finally prodded into celebrating her nut-and-candy-selling grandmother. What does she learn from this experience that she feared would find her rejected, that she feared was too private and domestic for public consumption? That "people are the *same* all over," an utter denial of her own reality.

Compare any bland, inoffensive, unrealistic, and homogenizing reader to Evaline Ness's *Sam, Bangs and Moonshine* (Holt, Rinehart & Winston, 1966). This story is about Samantha, a fisherman's daughter, who had the reckless habit of lying. Her habit took the form of imagining that her mother was a mermaid, that her pets included a lion and a kangaroo, and that the ragged old rug by the door was a chariot drawn by dragons. Bangs, her cat, "talks" to her, and Thomas, her young friend, believes what she says. Sam cannot distinguish what her father calls "real" from "moonshine." Without thinking, Sam sends Thomas to Blue Rock in a hunt for the phantom mermaid and baby kangaroo. The tide rises, a storm sets in, and Sam, with a lump in her throat, realizes what she has done. Sam's father rescues Thomas while Sam waits, her mouth and eyes closed tight. The rescue is greeted with her sobs of relief. At the resolution, she has come to know the difference between real and moonshine, but her world is still not black and white, for she knows there is bad moonshine and good moonshine. She, as do her readers, recognizes ambiguity.

What a contrast there is between this tale of real loss and regret, of perceptual levels, of coming to terms with one's own responsibility in an ambiguous world, and the textbook versions of "moonshine" stories! For example, a popular reader includes a story about Magdalena, a girl in an accelerated class, who is told to deceive Spooky, a new girl in class. It is the school principal who requests the deception as a means of getting Spooky to conform to class expectations.

I do not want to sound like a booster for any author or publishing company. However, a number of books older children choose to read because they are filled with adventure, or insight, or something meaningful to them are mentioned in the next chapter. These books include the Judy Blume novels, C. S. Lewis novels, works such as *Mrs. Frisby and the Rats of Nimh*, the Laura Ingalls Wilder series, paperback romances, and more. The roster is not definitive. My intention is merely to make suggestions.

Our children are being taught to read in schools whose texts encourage elementary skills and simplistic content. Our children are asked to read from those books which most easily satisfy the demands of the mass market created in part by the intense competition among publishers for acceptance of their texts by hundreds of school districts. One way to satisfy the demands of mass marketing is to keep one's product aimed at some lowest common denominator, to keep one's product attractive to the widest audience and offensive to none, to make one's product acceptable and provocative of little or no criticism. The result in the textbook market is reading books which assume a stable family structure in the characters' lives, which assume that individuals have little responsibility or control over their own destinies but are somehow part of some system which works out in the end, and which assume that everyone is about the same and thus all have the same problems.

What is often absent in school texts aimed at the older ten-to-twelve-year-old child is stories whose content is mysterious or intriguing or about deceit, romance, family conflict, revenge, and envy. What is too often present in the school texts is the assumptions that adults and authority figures can save the day, that problems all get worked out in the end (usually a very short time), and that the greatest problems older children face are conforming to peer and parental expectations.

If school textbooks are not serving the psychological or literary needs of our children, perhaps this is as it should be. Perhaps the school's role is to perpetuate mass values in an uncritical way. If this is the case, parents should be aware that a child's interest in school reading programs may be significantly different from the child's interest in reading literature, if the literature option is made available at home and through regular visits to the library. Our children need the emotional and psychological support that children's literature can provide, and they need to want to read once they've learned how.

The discussion about the *content* of older children's textbooks and literature and its relationship to their cognitive and psychological development may seem tangential to the subject of the relationship between language experiences and linguistic development. It is not. Older children need to appreciate the uses to which language is put in order to appreciate the uses they can make of language themselves.

With younger children it is easy to see the relationships between reading and other language experiences and their own language development. One can hear the development of the complex English sentence. One can relish the invention of metaphor, pun, or malapropism which often arises from the encounter with new words and experiences discovered through reading.

With older children, the relationship of reading and language development is less obvious, because most of the rules of English have been internalized. Ten-to-twelve-year-old children know, however unconsciously, the phonology, morphology, and syntax of their language. What they still need to acquire, and are working at acquiring, is another dimension of language—a dimension called "style."

Older children know how to decode words in terms of sound, how to inflect verbs for time, how to pluralize nouns for number, and how to put words in the right order to communicate simple messages in English. What reading helps them do, on the linguistic and not psychological level now, is to recognize options among a variety of possible modes of expression. If a child reads, "The old man lived down the street," the child may well say, "So?" But if the child reads, "The old man, long assumed to be rich, lived down the street in a now dilapidated mansion," the child may be encouraged to pursue the story.

By reading books that are based on literary value rather than mere recognizable sentence structure, characters, and vocabulary, children encounter varieties of expression, stretch their sense of the meaning of words, ponder the ambiguities of both language and character, and are, we hope, made sensitive to modes of expression. Perhaps this is an uncommon example, but a twelve-year-old child, after watching a rerun of *Gone with the Wind,* was found in her room, book and dictionary in hand, working through the long tome. The narrative itself had prompted the desire to read. The difficulty of the prose posed only a momentary problem and served as a lesson in language and style as she tried to find out what happened to Rhett and Scarlet.

Reading is, for all the pessimism and criticism expressed in this chapter, an often-mentioned hobby on forms children fill out for camp and other activities. The child who finishes a book and says "that was neat/swell/interesting/funny" has discovered a source of pleasure and linguistic information unlike any other.

# 9: On Reading

References to the relationship between language development and reading have been made both explicitly and implicitly throughout this book. It is time to address the subject head on.

Learning to read is something like learning a second language. Children acquire their native tongue in stages. They learn its sounds, its morphology, and its syntax and have all three in hand by the time they enter school. As school children, they learn that language is not simply sounds put together in a special way to communicate meaning, but is also represented symbolically by marks on a piece of paper.

This new dimension contributes to their language skills in a variety of ways. On the simplest level, they read, as young children, books that are written in a simple vocabulary with simple sentence structure which serve to reinforce the language skills they have acquired before entering school. On the wider level, they learn that printed words can produce stories and documentaries that teach them about the world, give them information, and open up new ways of thinking.

Reading introduces children to the *forms* of language and to *content* that is meaningful.

Books have a formal structure. On the adult level, to cite an example, a writer might structure a story about a man's growing sense of morality and the possibility of spiritual rebirth around the formal elements of the seasons, the spring bringing good news and the winter bad. Such a feat was accomplished in Bernard Malamud's *The Assistant*. Children's books are not necessarily so self-consciously form-and-content-related, but form is an important part of the writer's concern. One does not write in complex sentences if one's audience is a child who has just mastered the noun/verb/object sentence pattern, nor does one write about complex peer-group relationships if one's audience is a first-grader who has just begun to release basic family ties. On the other hand, one does not write about baby animals at a make-believe tea party in simple sentences to an audience of twelve-year-olds who have mastered the complex, imbedded sentence.

To reach an audience successfully and to entertain and charm that audience, books must suit their audience in terms of both form and content. The books I discuss in this chapter were chosen because of their author's sensitivity to the role of formal language elements and semantic, meaningful content at various age levels.

Several other principles of selection are in operation here. First, although categorizing books seemed the clearest way to present these recommendations, the reader must be aware that categories are neither inclusive nor exclusive; they are merely handy. A book recommended in one place might just have well been recommended in another; for example, Shel Silverstein's work in the group on metaphor could as easily have been placed in the group on humor. Second, although some real effort was made to make the recommendations up-to-date, the effort was defeated by a lingering love of some of the classics in child literature. Thus, the reader will find references to old books that are, however, still in print, as well as to books written in the 1980s. Third, the reader will notice that although many books are listed, not as many authors are. There is a reason for this. By citing a series of books by a single author, I have hoped to accomplish two things: to present options for the selection of valuable reading material, and to encourage parents and children alike to collect books. A random book here and there does not provide the same experience as the immersion into a style or form established by a given writer. Moreover, immersing oneself in a series of texts lends itself to collection and makes the question "What book do you want to read next?" easier to answer.

## Books for Younger Children

Young children have been characterized already as masters of the simple sentence, still delighted by the sounds of language, beginning to make and understand metaphors, and particularly interested in stories with animals personified and retold fairy tales and folk tales.

1. Books whose content is simple and whose language forms follow the structure of the basic English sentence are not hard to find and are frequently subtitled "An I-can-read book." These books encourage the child to do his own reading and include several authors, among many others, who seem to succeed at reaching children at this level.

Else Holmelund Minarik has written a series of books for young children about a little bear. Among them are *A Kiss for Little Bear* (1968), *Father Bear Comes Home* (1959), *Little Bear* (1957), *Little Bear's Friend* (1960), and *Little Bear's Visit* (1961), all published by Harper & Row.

Ludwig Bemelman's many *Madeline* books are also at this level, although the setting for them may be a bit foreign for many children. Among the books are the Penguin editions of *Madeline* (1977), *Madeline's Rescue* (1977), *Madeline and the Bad Hat* (1979), *Madeline and the Gypies* (1977) and *Madeline in London* (1971).

The *Frances* stories are also favorites at this level. Written by Russell Hoban and published by Harper & Row, the series includes *A Birthday for Frances* (1976) and *Bread and Jam for Frances* (1964).

Ezra Jack Keats is another author worth mentioning, for he follows the basic English sentence, writes stories with relatively simple messages, and often features non-Caucasian children. His book list includes *Goggles* (Macmillan, 1971), *The Snowy Day* (Viking, 1962), *Whistle for Willie* (Penguin, 1977), and *Jennie's Hat* (Harper & Row, 1966).

2. Books which depend more on sound than sense are still attractive to beginning readers and early elementary students. The clear favorite author in this category is Dr. Seuss, whose fifty and more titles include *Cat in the Hat* (Houghton Mifflin, 1957), *Green Eggs and Ham* (Beginner, PLB, 1960), *The Grinch Who Stole Christmas* (Random House, 1957), *Horton Hatches the Egg* (Random House, 1940), *Fox in Sox* (Random House, 1965), and *The Cat in the Hat Comes Back* (Random House, 1958). These stories trip off the tongue of both parent and child alike.

Not as well known as Dr. Seuss is Leonard Baskin, mainly an illustrator, whose *Hosie's Alphabet* (Viking Press, 1972) is a treasure of sounds. Although the text supplies neither simple syntax nor content, as it is an alphabet book, the examples for the letters are near tongue-twisters. For *G* he provides "a ghastly garrulous gargoyle," for *Q* "the quintessential quail," for *P* "the primordial protozoa." These samples stretch the child's vocabulary and are, in part, metaphoric.

3. Books that depend for meaning upon the understanding of metaphor are often too difficult for young children to read to themselves. That is, they do not have a long text, but the text is no longer written in simple sentences. Instead, the form becomes more complex, as does the subject. Third-graders, however, have no trouble with this kind of book, for they have begun to learn how to construct the complex or imbedded sentence and their concerns for acceptance, nonconformity, solitude, or companionship are up to the content level of books such as those written by Leo Lionni. Lionni often celebrates the poet, the nonconformist, the person with a sense of community and solidarity in such books as *In the Rabbitgarden, Inch by Inch, Tico and the Golden Wings, The Biggest House in the World, Alexander the Wind-up Mouse, Frederick, Swimmy,* and *Fish Is Fish,* most published by Pantheon in the 1970s.

Obviously, the real makers of metaphor are poets, and poetry, because of both its sounds and its metaphors, should be included at this level. I would suggest the Joan Anglund Walsh books such as *Spring Is a New Beginning*, (Harbrace, 1963), Gwendolyn Brooks's *The Tiger Who Wore White Gloves* (Third World, 1974), John Ciardi's *I Met a Man* (Houghton Mifflin, 1961), M. Sendak's *Chicken Soup with Rice* (Harper & Row, 1962), any number of anthologies of children's poetry, and the wonderful books of verse by Shel Silverstein *(Light in the Attic* and *Where the Sidewalk Ends)* included in the section on older children and humor.

Maurice Sendak's books, which include *In the Night Kitchen* (Harper & Row, 1970) and *Where the Wild Things Are* (Harper & Row, 1963), are not specifically books that make and deal with metaphors. What they do is create a symbolic environment in which a child can work out fears, fantasies, responsibilities, and such, and they should be included here. I recommend Sendak's work as highly as anyone's in this context.

4. Some books with animals personified have already been mentioned, for as explained earlier, categories are not as clear-cut as an organizer of a chapter might want them to be. Highly recommended in this category are the *Babar* books written by Jean de Brunhoff and his son, Laurent. Among the titles published by Random House in inexpensive hardbound editions are *The Story of Babar, Babar the King, The Travels of Babar, Babar's Birthday Surprise, Babar and the Wully Wully, Babar's Mystery,* and *Babar's Fair,* most reissued in the 1970s.

Three other authors are important in this context, the first because of her classic style of prose and picture and the latter two because of their sense of rascality, a theme to which I return in discussing the longer narrative for the older child.

Beatrix Potter has delighted children for years with her stories of Peter Rabbit, Mopsy, Flopsy, and Cottontail. She continues to do so. Her works are available from Frederick Warne, in hardcover miniatures.

H. A. Rey has written a series of *Curious George* books, about a monkey who can ride a bike, perform circus acts, and get into incredible trouble. Among Rey's dozen titles are *Curious George* (1941), *Curious George Rides a Bike* (1952), and *Curious George Goes to the Hospital* (1966), all published by Houghton Mifflin.

Michael Bond has written a series of books about a London bear named Paddington. Among his titles are *Paddington at Large* (1970), *More About Paddington* (1970), *Paddington Helps Out* (1970), *A Bear Called Paddington* (1968) and *Paddington at Work* (1971), all published by Dell under the Yearling imprint.

Although marketing emphases change from year to year, it has been interesting to note that over the past few years, all three of these fictional characters—Peter Rabbit, Curious George, and Paddington—have been featured as stuffed animals in department stores across the country, perhaps as a result of the books' popularity with young readers and listeners.

Another series of animal books that young children can read are published by the National Geographic Society. They are documentary, rather than narrative. The text is short, expressed in simple sentences, and illustrated by photographs. Some titles in the society's vast series are *Creatures of the Night, Wonders of the Desert World, Namu: Making Friends with a Killer Whale, The Blue Whale, Animals That Build Their Homes, How Animals Hide, Dogs Working for People, Wild Ponies, Honeybees, Pandas,* and *Creepy Crawly Things,* all published between 1970 and 1980 and available by subscription to the society.

5. Young children are also interested in fairy tales and retold folk tales, many of which were discussed in Chapter 7. The selection of fairy-tale editions is at the discretion of parents, but for background information plus the text of the tale itself, one might consider Iona and Peter Opie's *The Classic Fairy Tales* (Oxford University Press, 1974), an illustrated text which provides the historical background for variations in twenty-four of the most popular fairy tales.

When it comes to retold folk tales, my favorite is Tomie de Paola, a fine illustrator and stylist, whose books include *The Clown of God* (Scholastic Books, 1978), *Big Anthony and the Mag-*

*ic Ring* (Harcourt Brace Jovanovich, 1976), and *Strega Nona* (Prentice-Hall 1975).

Not quite a fairy tale or a folk tale, *Gustav the Gourmet Giant* (who finally concocts a recipe for boy soup) by LouAnn Gaeddert (Dial Press, 1976) is a must for any parent with an overweight, overeating child.

As a bridge, older children are more inclined to read realistic fiction within a much more elaborate and longer narrative form. Yet younger children, too, often prefer narratives about children like themselves to those that feature talking animals and mythical characters. They cannot handle the narrative length of a novel, but there are several realistic stories available to them. Two favorites are Evaline Ness's *Sam, Bangs and Moonshine* (Holt, Rinehart & Winston, 1966) and the *Alexander* books written by Judith Viorst and published by Atheneum. *Alexander and the Terrible, Horrible, No Good, Very Bad Day* (1976) and *Alexander Who Used to Be Rich Last Sunday* (1980) are both realistic and humorous.

## Books for Older Children

Older children have already been characterized as makers of malapropisms and humorists, concerned with the distinctions between fact and fancy. They are sophisticated enough in their use of complex language to understand long narrative works of literature, the three dominant kinds of narratives being adventure stories, realistic fiction, and romances. The first-mentioned linguistic phenomenon, the making of malapropisms, cannot be addressed in this chapter because it is not something any parent or teacher would want to encourage. Instead, malapropism may well be corrected, rather than encouraged, by increasing children's vocabularies through having them read books.

1. Older children delights in jokes, riddles, and puns. They come to this delight because of an awareness of the ambiguity of language and, often, of the human condition. There are so many

joke and riddle books on the market that selecting any few for inclusion here presents an insurmountable problem. But inasmuch as jokes and riddles are nearly the reverse side of poetry, which also depends upon distinctions of literal and figurative meaning, the inclusion here of two kinds of poetry books that are very funny seems appropriate. First, one might introduce children to the limerick, which is poetic in form, but humorous and punning in content (a caution here: Many limerick books on the market are more than a little risqué and suggestive). Second, one cannot go far wrong in directing the jokester to the poetic works of Shel Silverstein. His *Where the Sidewalk Ends* (Harper & Row 1974) and *A Light in the Attic* (Harper & Row, 1981), rhyme, play on words, and deal with subjects pertinent to the older child. A list of some of his poems makes this clear: "Sarah Cynthia Sylvia Stout Would Not Take the Garbage Out," "Poem on the Neck of a Running Giraffe," "Recipe for a Hippopotamus Sandwich," and "Hector the Collector" are but a few.

2. Concerned about the distinction between fact and fancy—but not always sure what they really prefer—children often are intrigued by fanciful facts. A shoo-in favorite book around my home is the *Guinness Book of World Records,* which holds the attention and amazes children for hour on end. The fattest man, the thinnest waist, the longest mustache, the fastest sprint, the "most of" anything makes children nearly incredulous—and yet, it's true.

When they do turn from fact back into fantasy they have some wonderful options. C. S. Lewis wrote a series of novels called the *Chronicles of Narnia* (Collier Books, most recent edition 1978), which include seven short novels: *The Lion, the Witch and the Wardrobe, Prince Caspian, The Voyage of the Dawn Treader, The Silver Chair, The Horse and His Boy, The Magician's Nephew,* and *The Last Battle.* E. B. White's *The Trumpet of the Swan* (Harper & Row, 1970) tells the tale of a trumpeter swan who is defective and cannot signal to his love until his father gives him a trumpet to aid him through his life. *Mrs. Frisby and the Rats of*

*Nimh,* by Robert C. O'Brien (Scholastic Books, 1971), explores the relationship of a simple rat to the human community that annoys her and a race of superintelligent rats who come to her aid. Kenneth Grahame's *Wind in the Willows* remains a classic for this age group and their interests, as do Saint-Exupéry's *The Little Prince* and J.R.R. Tolkien's *The Hobbit,* available from Ballantine in a nicely illustrated 1978 paperback edition.

Not recommended, but certainly in this category of books that may be fact and may be fiction, are ghost and horror stories from which so many recent movies have been made. Don't be surprised if a child from ten to twelve sneaks home a copy of *Carrie, Dracula, Alien,* or *The Exorcist.* In most cases, the language is beyond them, but the curiosity for this kind of tale is certainly present.

3. Most of the long narratives suggested for children between the ages of ten and twelve fall into one of three general categories. They are adventure stories that particularly emphasize the out-of-doors, animals, or fantastic events. Or they are realistic in that they emphasize current issues in preadolescent life, are based on some actual historical situation, or create characters who have a bit of the rascal about them. Or they are somewhat realistic romances that celebrate boy-meets-girl situations and deal with prepubescent sexuality.

Most of the adventure stories addressed to this age group seem, whatever the women's movement might say, directed to boy readers. To cite several authors, Jim Kjelgaard has written a long series of books about wildlife and animals that are popular from generation to generation. Among his titles, most of which have been reprinted since their 1950-60 original publication by Bantam and Scholastic, are *Two Dogs and a Horse, Irish Red, Lion Hound, Big Red, Stormy, Outlaw Red,* and *Wild Trek.* They are in many ways the child's Jack London novels.

Another popular adventure/animal/outdoors series has been made more so by the recent release of the movie *The Black Stallion,* a film based on the dozens of *Black Stallion* books written by Walter Farley, published by Random House in the late 1970s.

In 1981 a whole new concept in adventure writing hit the paperback book market. Bantam Books and authors Edward Packard, D. Terman, and L. A. Montgomery produced a series of books called *Choose Your Own Adventure* that give plot twists and conclusion as options to the reader. I cannot attest to their literary value, but I have seen nonreaders become readers simply because of this gimmick of choice. Among the dozen or so titles are *The Lost Jewels of Nabooti*, *The Third Planet from Altair*, *Your Code Name Is Jonah*, *The Mystery of Chimney Rock*, and *By Balloon to the Sahara*.

Before moving on, parents and teachers should be reminded that "current" doesn't always mean best. As stories that grip the imagination and have exciting plots, the *Hardy Boys* and *Nancy Drew* mystery series are still available.

Realistic fiction takes several forms. It can emphasize current issues in preadolescent life. This is the function and, I would guess, the reason for the popularity of the Judy Blume novels, again books that have made readers out of nonreaders. Blume seems to address ten-to-fourteen-year-old girls, in particular, right where they live. Among her titles are *Otherwise Known as Sheila the Great* (Dutton, 1972), *Tiger Eyes* (Bradbury Press, 1981), and *Starring Sally Freedman as Herself, Are You There God? It's Me, Margaret, Tales of a Fourth Grade Nothing*, and *It's Not the End of the World*, all published by Dell in 1977.

Also in this category is Peggy Mann's *My Dad Lives in a Downtown Hotel* (Doubleday, 1973), and the Pippi Longstocking series written by Astrid Lingren and published by Viking Press. Other talented outsiders who don't quite conform are featured in Ursula Le Guin's *Very Far Away from Anywhere Else* (Bantam, 1979). Incidentally, she has also written a trilogy of realistic/fantastic books called *The Earthsea Trilogy*, which includes *A Wizard of Earthsea*, (Bantam, 1975), *The Tombs of Atuan* (Bantam, 1975), and *The Farthest Shore* (Bantam, 1975).

Realistic fiction can also be based on some actual historical situation. It can create characters that continue to live in our imagination after many years have passed since they were created, or it can create settings in the past to which readers can nonetheless relate. The most famous series in this context would seem to be the series created by Laura Ingalls Wilder, which includes such titles as *The Little House on the Prairie, By the Shores of Silver Lake, Farmer Boy, The Long Winter, Little House in the Big Woods,* and *On the Banks of Plum Creek,* reprinted in matching editions by Harper & Row in 1971.

L. M. Montgomery's series, which includes *Anne of Green Gables, Anne of Avonlea,* and *Anne of the Island,* originally published in 1909 but reissued by Bantam Books in 1981, is another example of popular realistic fiction.

Accounts of memorable figures from the past, especially if those figures are young, are also of interest to children. Two that come immediately to mind are *The Diary of Anne Frank* (Pocket Books, 1955) and Esther Forbes's *Johnny Tremain* (Dell, 1969).

If one turns to the classics, one finds Tom Sawyer up to no end of mischief, Huck Finn breaking the law, *Little Women*'s Jo breaking social norms, Eloise destroying the organization of a hotel, and so on. Current literature does not differ much from the classics. Rarely is the major character a pure and true angel. Instead, major characters tend, as does Wilma in Vera Cleaver's *Queen of Hearts* (Bantam, 1980), to disobey crotchety grandmothers, or to behave mischievously and to receive dire punishments in the best of all possible worlds, as in Roald Dahl's *The Chocolate Factory* (Knopf, 1973), and to make long-distance calls to Australia from Dad's office in Viorst's *Alexander and the Terrible, Horrible, No Good, Very Bad Day* (Atheneum, 1972).

Finally, older children find romances appealing, especially female readers to whom the adventure series seem not to appeal. I will list none of them here, since I cannot recommend their content. They are the junior level of the Harlequin Romances, and although not offensive or outright sexual, they are formulaic and not particularly interesting.

Many fine authors have been skipped over in this listing, but my intent is simply to give parents, teachers, and readers a place from which to begin to discover reading materials within the formal reach of children (that is, within their ability to process the vocabulary, to understand the sentence forms, and to identify with the subject matter).

These books also have content material which appeals to various age levels from six through twelve. And at this point I offer a bit of a disclaimer. Content is very important to our children's perceptions of their world and their experience, but there have been many times in many of our lives when we wouldn't care what our children read, just as long as they read. In this context I suggest that all of us remember the reading of billboards, comic strips and comic books, and even cereal boxes. A skill learned is a skill learned.

# 10: On Writing

A reservation seems in order as we begin this last chapter. I have taught reading and writing for the past eighteen years, and, although my teaching has been to college-age students, the patterns of learning do not seem to vary. I have worked in the field of child language for nearly a decade, read most of the available literature in the field, conducted (often with the assistance of able graduate students) various field studies of children's acquisition of sounds, morphology, syntax, and semantical concepts, and written in the area of both child language acquisition and grammatical theory. Invariably, those studies touched on reading and writing, because a child learning language is a child learning to read and write, and the areas of acquisition are not clearly separate. Thus, without claiming to be an expert on reading and writing, I would like to make some suggestions about:

1. what seems to be the relationship between reading and writing, and writing and the development of language skills;

2. games that encourage vocabulary building, spelling, and language skills that are the building blocks of writing;

3. encouraging children to enjoy and develop their "private voices" through the keeping of journals and diaries;

4. a formal plan for learning to write that parents may not want to put into practice because it takes so much consistent time to develop, but that teachers may want to adapt for classroom work; and

5. an editorial, rewriting technique called "sentence combining" that has become the rave of many public school curriculum developers and has worked successfully in the classrooms of many teachers.

The relationship between reading and writing seems symbiotic, but there is still no hard and fast evidence that a good and avid reader is likely to be a technically good writer. The arguments, nonetheless, seem to favor the position that if one reads a lot, one will be a better writer. This seems to be true for two reasons.

First, a potential writer who is also a reader is exposed to various levels of writing if her reading list ranges from the backs of cereal boxes to classics in literature. Although most children are not self-conscious about what they read, an alert parent or teacher can use these reading variables to encourage learning about language choice, word selection, and style.

For instance, a child who is touched by the sense of abandonment that arises from the death of a parent or a divorce in a family that she has read about in a popular adolescent novel may be encouraged to read a more classic, perhaps finer, piece of literature on the same subject. She may move beyond pulp fiction picked up in the grocery store check-out lane to *Anne of Green Gables* or even *Huckleberry Finn*. Discovering that the treatment of a given subject may vary widely from writer to writer is one way children are introduced to style and excellence, to the understanding that the mode of expression is an important part of the meaning of what is read.

Second, a potential writer must have something to write about. The old adage seems to hold true. One does not write writing. Instead, one writes about something—and very often that something is modeled on what one has read or experienced. As parents and teachers alike will remember, early compositions about "winter" were much harder to write "in general" than they were after reading about a snowbound family in Vermont or a blizzard endured by the Ingalls family. Accurate descriptions of Uncle Hank, the hero of the day, were often easier to write after reading about Johnny Tremain's adventures during the Revolutionary War, and for the same reason: A potential writer needs models, for no creativity arises in a vacuum. Of course, by models, I do not mean that writers should copy others (although copying an exact text is a good exercise in accuracy and spelling), just that forms to follow provide guidelines for the beginning writer.

For example, most beginning writers depend for their content on people they have known, places they have visited, or events they have experienced. Reading samples of such recollections can provide models for the young writer. Biographies, travelogues, and histories written for children can provide this impetus.

Potential writers—whether children or adults—cannot even begin the feat without the rudiments of the writer's craft, such as spelling, word choice, diction, a sense of connotation and denotation, and vocabulary. With children, an easy and fun way to develop such word sensitivities is through play, a theme that has been emphasized throughout this text. There are many commercial and homemade word games that can sensitize children to language. I mention just a few here.

Three commercial games that encourage language and writing skills are Scrabble, crossword puzzles, and find-a-word books. Scrabble is a vocabulary-building game that depends upon spelling and dictionary skills. It is available in both junior and adult versions. The adult version seems to work with elementary school children, if adults become partners with the children. In fact, such an arrangement makes the game family-oriented, demonstrating both generations' enthusiasm for language. Crossword puzzles are available at many levels and need no more than a mention. Find-a-word books are available at most bookstores, groceries, and variety stores and encourage word recognition and spelling skills.

Two homemade games that do the same are hangman and

list-a-word. Hangman is a classic guessing game. You must guess a word chosen by your opponent by guessing which letters the word contains before erroneous guesses "hang" you. (For the first error, your opponent draws a head in a noose, then the neck, then the torso, and so on.) Hangman encourages spelling, and a sense of the frequency of letters in English words (for example, an *e* is always a better guess than *x*).

List-a-word, which may have other names of which I am unaware, is a favorite party game. To play, each child receives a piece of paper (numbered 1-20, 1-50, or whatever has been decided) which has the same phrase or word on the top, a phrase such as "Christmas Joy" or "Incredible Hulk." The task is to see who can, within a timed period, find all the little words that can be made from it. For instance "Christmas Joy" will produce "cat," "mast," "jot," "sot," "sat," "sit," "smart," "hit," "hat," "hot," "rims," "say," and many, many more. This game encourages spelling, word recognition, and morphological sophistication—the knowledge that certain sounds combine in English to make words and others do not.

Besides becoming sensitive to vocabulary and word choice—with all that implies for subtle shades of meaning—potential writers also have to distinguish between various kinds of voices. One kind of voice relates to a point of view or narrative position. In the first-person narrative, "I" tell the story. In the third-person narrative, every character is depicted as "he" or "she" or "Frank" or "Jenny" by someone who knows the thoughts and speaks with the voice of everybody in the tale.

But "voice" also means something different that concerns me more. Potential writers—as inclined to be children as anyone else—can learn the difference between the private and public voice, the voice that is "themselves talking to themselves" and the voice that is "themselves talking to others." In the first case, the voice is self-expressive and is not necessarily communicative. Given no audience, there is no need to be careful to translate felt emotions into understood experience. In the second case, the voice is trying to communicate felt emotions so that another person can respond in kind.

One way in which children can be made sensitive to the importance and quality of their private voices is by encouraging them to keep diaries and travel journals.

Diaries somehow appeal more to girls than to boys, but there is no real reason for this. Diaries that can be locked and kept as tantalizing objects for siblings and parents alike should appeal to children of both sexes. The important thing about diaries is to ensure their confidentiality and to encourage their use on an everyday basis. The habit of writing—whether about important matters, or about what one had to eat on a given day—is the habit of writing. Once it is begun, it becomes part of the daily ritual, an automatic behavior.

Journals are a little more specialized. Not locked up, they can be used by the whole family to remember trips, in particular. Journals too provide daily writing experience and can be used to chronicle those things that are important to children. I always keep a journal of car, hotel, and food expenses when we travel, so my children see me writing several times a day. One of my children is an architecture freak and notes buildings, pastes in postcards of buildings, and comments about the places where favorite buildings are located. Another child is food-conscious and writes down names of restaurants, meals ordered, and delights therein encountered. The subject of the journal seems to make no difference as long as the daily experience of writing is exercised.

Journals can be made from the most inexpensive tablets and notebooks to be found at discount stores and variety stores, but to encourage the importance of journal-keeping, parents might think about the value of buying a cloth-bound journal, available at most bookstores and department stores. Quality of materials may well encourage quality of content.

As a bridge from the private to the more public voice, letters can encourage children to write. Letters can vary from the most casual and brief thank-you note for gifts to extended letters to foreign pen pals. Content seems to matter less than does the experience of writing down one's thank-you's, activities, or feelings.

Many schools and many school publications, such as *The Weekly Reader,* have lists of pen pals available for children, or addresses from which one might obtain such a list. Children met on summer vacations or at camp, children of parents' friends, and relatives who live some distance away are also good audiences for letter writers.

Parents need a caution here, however. Increasingly, in the hectic and electronic world in which we live, even adults don't write letters. Instead, we pick up the phone and make long-distance calls, excused because we are too busy to sit down and write a letter. The excuse may be valid, but the example that is being set may not be the one that is best for our children, if we want them to take time to write.

To provide a bridge that extends even further from the private voice to the public voice of written discourse, children at the journal- and letter-writing stage can be taught how to "immortalize" their private recollections, to move from being journal keepers to being "memorists."

Elementary school children don't usually have a wealth of experience upon which to draw in trying to write about people, places, and events, the most common subjects of memoir writing. Nonetheless, they can be asked to describe a favorite aunt, a favorite restaurant, or a memorable birthday party. The trick in encouraging memoir writing is to move the child past generalizations and into a sense of detailed description, an exercise that reinforces what the child already knows about the power of adjectives and certain verbs.

For instance, most children, like most adults, would describe Aunt Sally as "pretty and nice and funny," a favorite restaurant as having "super hamburgers and lots of french fries," and a memorable birthday party as "fun." What children who would be writers must move past are these abstractions that *summarize* an experience rather than *present* it. They need to be encouraged to paint with words, to describe a person, place, or event in such detail that the reader feels he is there. Children who would be writers need to learn how to describe Aunt Sally so that the reader says to himself, "My, doesn't she sound pretty, nice, and funny." Or says of the restaurant, "My, isn't that a nice place to go for delicious food." Or says of the birthday party, "What a joyful day that must have been."

In order for the reader to say those things, rather than having the writer say them for him, the writer must describe and paint pictures. For instance, Aunt Sally's blue eyes and dimpled smile which shows just a tiny space between her teeth must be rendered, as should some activity of generosity such as her rising early in the morning to sew sequins on a child's dancing costume. Some incident should reveal her sense of humor. The same things are true of the description of place and event. They must be rendered in order for them to be truly descriptive and memorable.

This kind of exercise in descriptive writing can be encouraged on the "pre-writing" level as well, to borrow a term from rhetorician W. Ross Winterowd (*The Contemporary Writer*, Harcourt Brace Jovanovich, 1981). Thus, children who respond "stuff" when asked what they learned in school today can be encouraged to say more so their audience can understand what "stuff" means.

An expansion of the memoir or descriptive piece that is, in turn, an extension of the private voice into a more public forum is found in the writing of narrative or fiction. Because elementary school children are involved in reading of one kind or another they can be taught to emulate various forms of the short story and poem, even the novel, although most children between the ages of six and twelve have neither the attention span nor the motor skills to write a very long piece. Most school curricula include these kinds of exercises, so parents, in most cases, need only encourage their children's attempts at rhyming verse, making up metaphors, or writing fantasies.

More difficult to do, and requiring more formal work, is instructing the child writer in prose forms that will really be required only in academic situations. If parents wish to prepare their children for high school and college writing, they can teach writing forms that require comparison or contrast (both of which involve a sense of organization, metaphor and the seeing or likenesses and dissimilarities, and category), and explain cause or process (both of which involve a sense of logic and cause-effect relationships). As the attentive reader will notice, these are cognitive and linguistic concepts that children are picking up along the way and are, thus, not beyond them. What may be beyond them is the patience to learn how to express these concepts and relationships without thinking that learning to write in these modes is a veritable pain. What may be beyond parents who elect to introduce their children to these modes is an explanation of why the children should learn these kinds of expressions. I leave motivation up to the individual mentor and offer some subject suggestions instead.

Children who are developing a sense of metaphor and category, which most of them do in the early elementary grades, almost intuitively see the relationships between things, as did the little girl who, after brushing into a prickly bush, exclaimed that it was "a bumblebee tree." Given this developing ability that seems nearly intuitive, then, one can work with self-conscious expressions of such similarities and dissimilarities. One might ask a child to compare a daisy and a rose, encouraging the child to write about their needs for water and nutrients, their similar reactions to sun, their organization as complex organisms of stem, leaves, stamen, pistil, blossom, and seed. In reverse, one might encourage a child to write about the flowers' dissimilarities, hoping that she will notice the thorns on one, the variation of petal formation, the differences in color and smell, and so on.

Children who are developing a sense of the relationship of real and unreal, of the relationships of actions and consequences, and of time, space, dimension, and reciprocity are apt candidates for writing in academic forms. These somewhat older children could be asked to write down the directions for baking a cake, making tacos, preparing various kinds of hamburgers, etc. Or children might be asked to explain in writing how they get to school, how they attach the wheels to a model airplane, or how they sew on a button. Again, the parent or teacher who is guiding this activity must be alert to steer the children from overgeneralizations and abstractions and get the children to be as specific and detailed as they can be. "You stir up this stuff, put it in a pan, and bake it" does not explain the process by which one bakes a cake.

Children also might be encouraged to explain the relationships between electrical storms and power outages, matches and fires, good behavior and movie privileges. Each of these topics requires children to express what they know about cause and effect and the logic behind common rules.

Once children begin to write—whether journals, diaries, letters, or small essays that approximate descriptive, comparative, contrastive, causal, and processive tasks that really won't be expected of them until they are further along in school—they can be introduced to a technique that has caught on in school system after school system, classroom after classroom. This is a writing/editing technique called *sentence combining*. My experiences in using this technique with fourth and eighth graders and with college freshmen has been amazingly successful. As experts in sentence combining I would cite the author of *Sentence Combining*, William Strong (Random House, 1973), and Dr. Nicholas J. Karolides of the University of Wisconsin–River Falls, whose work with upper elementary children I noted in *Baby Talk* (New American Library, 1978). The following exercises suggest the training in style and polish that the technique provides.

Most elementary school children, although they are learning the complex patterns of the English sentence—patterns that enable them to ask questions, make negative statements, substitute pronouns for other nouns, change the tenses of verbs to more clearly signal meaning, and combine sentences one into another for compressed and creative expression—do not always use these patterns when they write. Although they are learning how to transform the basic English sentence into something more complex when they speak, their writing often reads like a first-grade primer. For example, a child writing a short composition about the similarities between the daisy and the rose, mentioned earlier, might well write:

> The daisy and the rose both have stems.
> The daisy and the rose both have leaves.
> The daisy and the rose both need water and sunlight.
> The daisy and the rose both have blossoms.
> Only one of the flowers smells really sweet.

The sentence-combinging technique teaches children how to immerse one or more of these sentences into another, by converting one or more of the sentences into adjective phrases or subordinate clauses. (Note that children don't need to know the terms in order to understand the process.)

The simplest kind of sentence combining involves joining sentences and parts of sentences with conjunctions. Thus, an easy combining might produce: "Both the daisy and the rose have stems, leaves, and blossoms."

This combination doesn't do much for the remaining two sentences, but with a little manipulation children will come to see that by subordinating one sentence to another, the two can be combined in the production of: "Although both need water and sunlight, only one has a sweet smell." Although the child's composition is now reduced from five sentences to two, the two that remain are stylistically stronger and more lively.

One way to begin teaching this technique is to let children pre-write by simply listing one simple sentence after another that attempts to describe whatever their subject is, then direct them to recognize the similarity in various kinds of sentence patterns which lend themselves to combination, and then to let them experiment with ways of combining seemingly disparate sentences without changing the intended meaning. This technique has been remarkably successful in sensitizing children to the possibilities of language manipulation, choice, style, and more.

To conclude, children are inventors and creators of language, as evidenced in studies of their speech, their stories, their jokes, their interest in reading, and their ability to learn to write. They'll learn in spite of us, but if we understand the tasks they have set themselves to accomplish, we can ease the way and encourage what delights us all—original and honest expression.

# SELECTED BIBLIOGRAPHY

Beck, M. Susan. *Baby Talk* (New American Library, 1973).

A book addressed to parents, educators, and child psychologists based on the theories of Noam Chomsky. It deals with the development of language in children from eighteen months to six years, emphasizing phonology, morphology, and syntax and the predictable order in which the acquisition of each occurs.

Bettelheim, Bruno. *The Uses of Enchantment* (Knopf, 1976).

A book addressed to a literate audience particularly interested in fairy tales. Its theory adds a Freudian and psychic dimension to the reader's understanding of the meaning of fairy tales.

Brown, Roger. *A First Language* (Harvard University Press, 1973).

A rather technical book which deals with the studies of early language done with Eva, Sara, and others in the Harvard area. The book is filled with linguistic-language, but is valuable for its thorough analysis of the time schedule children seem to adhere to in learning the elements of language. Particularly helpful is the section on the acquisition of morphological elements.

Chomsky, Noam. *Syntactic Structure* (The Hague: Mouton, 1957).

      *Aspects of a Theory of Syntax* (MIT Press, 1965).

 Both technical linguistic studies that address scholars and others familiar with the language of linguistic analysis. Of wider and deeper interest are:

      *Language and Mind* (Harcourt, Brace: 1968).
      *Reflections on Language* (Pantheon, 1975).

 Both deal with language and its relationship to theories of learning and the mind. They are philosophical and readable, extending linguistic study far beyond the concern for noun and verb agreement.

 Even further from simply linguistic analyses are three books which deal with the relationships between langauge and social freedom and responsibility:

      *Language and Responsibility* (Pantheon, 1977).
      *Problems of Knowledge and Freedom* (Pantheon, 1971).
      *Reasons of State* (Pantheon, 1971, 1973).

Dale, Philip S. *Language Development: Structure and Function,* 2nd ed. (Holt, Rinehart & Winston, 1976).

 Accessible to some readers, as it is not as linguistically technical as either Brown or Chomsky. The book includes many good examples, summarized charts from the more technical works of others, and explained experiments. Readers with no linguistic preparation may find this a little difficult.

de Villiers, Jill and Peter. *Language Acquisition* (Harvard University Press, 1978).

 Better organized that the Dale book cited above, but with the same difficulties. This book has some very interesting and readable chapters on the child's acquisition of semantics, a

# Selected Bibliography / 115

subject very rarely included in such books. It also does a nice job of summarizing the research of others, particularly of Susan Carey, not otherwise listed here.

Goodman, Yetta and Kenneth. *Miscue Analysis: Applications to Reading Instruction* (National Council of Teachers of English, 1973).

Hayakawa, S. I. *Language in Thought and Action* (Harcourt Brace Jovanovich, 1978).

No longer really current in linguistic/semantic theory, this book provides a highly readable introduction to a theory about language and its relationship to social behavior and attitude. It is not linguistically technical, but written in jargon-free language, as it explains the linguistic sources of prejudice, illogical and hasty judgment, and more.

Linden, Eugene. *Apes, Man and Language* (Penguin, 1976).

A book written for the mass market. This book deals with the studies of chimpanzee and ape language that have been conducted for the last decade. Very readable, although its descriptions of houses and experimental labs may seem a little overdone. The thesis of the book is that human and animal language systems may not be as far apart as we humans have liked to believe.

Lyon, John. *Semantics I* and *II* (London: Cambridge University Press, 1979).

Again, technical linguistics books. Neither pertains explicitly to the child's acquisition of semantics, but each provides a valuable summary and exploration of the current debate in linguistic research about semantic development.

McNeill, David. *The Acquisition of Language: The Study of Developmental Psycholinguistics* (Harper & Row, 1970).

Similar in terms of readability and content to the Philip S. Dale text mentioned above. This book also includes some very interesting comparisons between human and animal biology and language systems.

Steiner, George. *After Babel* (Oxford, 1975).

Sensitive, intelligent criticism of current linguistic theory, including that of Noam Chomsky.

# Index